DAVID WELLS'
PSYCHIC SECRETS

2019

DAVID WELLS'
PSYCHIC SECRETS

David Wells

HAY HOUSE

Australia • Canada • Hong Kong • India
South Africa • United Kingdom • United States

First published and distributed in the United Kingdom by:
Hay House UK Ltd, 292B Kensal Rd, London W10 5BE. Tel.: (44) 20
8962 1230; Fax: (44) 20 8962 1239. www.hayhouse.co.uk

Published and distributed in the United States of America by:
Hay House, Inc., PO Box 5100, Carlsbad, CA 92018-5100. Tel.: (1) 760
431 7695 or (800) 654 5126; Fax: (1) 760 431 6948 or (800) 650 5115.
www.hayhouse.com

Published and distributed in Australia by:
Hay House Australia Ltd, 18/36 Ralph St, Alexandria NSW 2015. Tel.:
(61) 2 9669 4299; Fax: (61) 2 9669 4144. www.hayhouse.com.au

Published and distributed in the Republic of South Africa by:
Hay House SA (Pty), Ltd, PO Box 990, Witkoppen 2068. Tel./Fax: (27)
11 467 8904. www.hayhouse.co.za

Published and distributed in India by:
Hay House Publishers India, Muskaan Complex, Plot No.3, B-2, Vasant
Kunj, New Delhi – 110 070. Tel.: (91) 11 4176 1620; Fax: (91) 11 4176 1630.
www.hayhouse.co.in

Distributed in Canada by:
Raincoast, 9050 Shaughnessy St, Vancouver, BC V6P 6E5. Tel.: (1)
604 323 7100; Fax: (1) 604 323 2600

© David Wells, 2009

A catalogue record for this book is available from the British Library.

ISBN 978-1-84850-159-1

All of the papers used in this product are recyclable, and made from
wood grown in managed, sustainable forests and manufactured at
mills certified to ISO 14001 and/or EMAS.

Printed in the UK by CPI William Clowes Beccles NR34 7TL

This book is dedicated to all of you
who sent an e-mail, asked a question,
came to a workshop and gave me a hug
when you saw me – without you there
really would be no point!

Contents

Preface

Secrets are odd things, aren't they? It's the fact that you know something nobody else knows that makes them so exciting – and frankly in this case pretty useless! I'm not one for keeping secrets when it comes to my spiritual journey, techniques and beliefs, but I guess calling this book 'David Wells' Psychic Shout Out' wouldn't have been so intriguing...

The truth is that in sharing some of my experiences I hope to give you the opportunity to unlock some of the secrets that are inside you, and once you do you will want to unlock more and more.

You are a divine being attempting to live an earthly life, and that isn't always easy, but remembering your connection to the divine can not only make it a smoother ride but also help you understand why you have chosen some of the challenges that have come your way and better manage some of those that are yet to come.

You are in fact a combination of divine and earthly, and you already know that secret, but, like most us, you may be looking for that personal proof that there really is something more to it all. Whether you choose to find it through looking for astrals on a ghost hunt or contacting your spiritual guides or finding out more about astrology or the Qabalah or healing, there are secrets in this book that will help you along the way. I hope there are some surprises for you, too, and some things that will make you stop and think. There may be a few things you don't agree with. That's just fine. We are all unique and from my point of view as long as you begin to see there is something more going on, that's enough for now.

Enjoy.

Acknowledgements

So many people help in so many different ways, and whether it's making a cup of tea or laughing at my panic and frustration, which always helps me get a grip, I thank you for it.

In particular I would like to thank those who have let me tell their story. In being brave enough to share some of their hard lessons, I am sure they will help others understand there's an answer.

SPECIAL THANKS TO:
My teacher Jenni Shell and my friend Jenny Greentree for their encouragement and calm influence.

Hay House for being just fantastic, and Michelle, Jo and Lizzie for their advice and very professional eyes.

My mates for letting me leave early, arrive late and have a face like a bulldog chewing a wasp – Lee, Jarvis, Mark, Andrew, Sue and Diane in particular.

My family, of course, without whom I would be lost.

Chapter 1

Paranormal, Psychic or Spiritual?

Don't we all come to our spiritual path through some awareness that there is more out there than is obvious? I know that when I was growing up I had a huge family and as uncles and grandparents passed I wondered what it was all about and wished I could see them again, or at least have some proof that they continued to exist. There are many ways in which that proof can come to us and they are all valid, be they paranormal, psychic or spiritual.

Paranormal events are usually defined as activities that are unexplained – things that go bump in the night. Some people choose to investigate them and this can literally open up other worlds. The local astral world is the first we will come across, it's the plane directly next to us if you like, therefore it stands to reason that it's the easiest to contact. Some people make that contact, in whatever way they choose, and that's enough; some stick there doing it time and time again; and others acknowledge it, learn from it and move on to other things on other planes and realms of existence. As always, it's a personal choice.

Psychic is generally a term for seeing the future, for those moments when the veil of time is thin and those who can use their ability to peer beyond it do just that. It's also a knowing – that moment when you recognize that there's more going on between some mates than a shared interest in knitting. There are many ways of seeing the future, and Tarot cards, astrology and all sorts of other things are wrapped up in it, but not exclusively – they are very much part of the next category, which is spirituality.

Spiritual is a confusing term. To be spiritual, do you have to sit cross-legged on the floor three times a day, munch mung beans and promise never to swear or raise your voice in public? Of course not – you are human and you will have moments when you may not act in a way that others consider spiritual. Which brings me to the question, is spirituality about the perception of others? Are you spiritual only if they say so? Again, of course not. And do you have to adhere to a particular practice in order to be spiritual? Not at all. If you love a good ghost walk and an incense stick, then good for you, so do I. If you can't make a move without your Tarot cards, then get on with it, and if you see angels surrounding you every day, then well done, you. If you don't, fine. It's not a competition. In fact it's nothing to do with others at all – it's *your* journey.

Enlightening Journeys

As you start to develop spiritually it's not always an easy journey. When I first started the Qabalah, I was getting on OK. I was doing what I thought you did. I was trying to have a relationship, buying a house, getting on with work and really wanting that promotion, because promotion meant more money, more status and a bigger name badge. As my teaching began I was expecting to see my guide, listen to my granny with more clarity and to have some magical experiences along the way – all of which I got, by the way, and with bells on – but actually what I was looking for all along was something completely different. What we truly seek isn't always obvious to us and some journeys start with a step that may not be on the road we actually want to walk.

When I look back at the young man who turned up for the Qabalah group on day one he seems to be someone else in many aspects, but when I look again I can see the core of who I am now and I can see the truth of what I was seeking. If only we could go back and tell ourselves what we know now!

So you may begin looking for evidence that your lost loved ones are all right or may want to find out if things really do go bump in the night, and then you might go on to think about how you can predict what's going to happen to your mates or even total strangers; but soon the universe and its awesome beauty and its immaculate plan will get a hold on you and sooner or later you will want to know who or what is at the beating heart of it all.

Through past lives, astrology, Tarot and Qabalah, a journey unfolded for me, but it's not your journey. I can tell you about my journey to help you along yours, but you have to take that trip for yourself. So how can you start? Simple. You start at the beginning.

Secret: Do something.

Not much of a secret, you may think – in fact, it sounds very obvious – but if you're not advancing because you're not doing anything then maybe it's the most important secret of all.

So what gets you motivated? How can you go from just joining in to standing out? How do you become the shepherd rather than one of the sheep?

Your belief system may be different from that of your friends or your family, but that doesn't mean you're any more right than they are horribly wrong, it just means you're different. Therefore just accept those differences and neither preach nor shy away from them, simply accept your family and friends as you hope they accept you.

Next it's time to get some structure in what you do. You can be a serial medium seeker, wrap yourself in purple and wait for the next white feather to fall to confirm your angels are with you or you can choose to get some strength through having a doctrine you resonate with. Of course I am going to suggest the Qabalah, because that worked for me, but I am also going to suggest Taoism, Buddhism, Christianity, Hinduism, Paganism, in fact any 'ism' you want to follow. Just take it and make it your own, bring your own unique sense of who you are to it. I meet many people on my travels and the ones who stand out, who light up a room, are those who have made their beliefs their own.

In order to do this, of course, you have to know yourself, and this is in fact the next secret I want to share with you...

Know Thyself

This is advice that has been passed down through the ages. It sounds good, doesn't it, but how *do* you truly know yourself?

Honesty.

Next question!

No, seriously, if you are honest about the way you are, you'll find there are many advantages to it, one immediate one being that you can act accordingly. If, say, you know you're a grumpy mare in the mornings, you may choose to avoid others until after your first coffee. If you have a tendency to say you will help someone out and then think, 'What have I done that for?' you may want to admit that you speak up too early and hold back a bit.

And that doesn't have to be the way you do it forever and ever, unless of course you want to. Because knowing yourself means knowing how you can change too.

It also means knowing what you want – what you really, really want. Learning how to discriminate between what you want and what you're getting into by just going along with things isn't easy to do, because you're usually attempting to break habits you have built up over years, if not centuries. But it's really worth a try.

Take a piece of paper and a pen. Actually, I know I say this all the time, but do have a journal as well – it really is indispensable when you're on any magical path.

Back to your pen and paper.

Draw a line down the centre of the paper and on the right-hand side put down:

○ *What* you just let happen when you say 'yes' when you actually mean 'no'.

○ *When* you go along with things rather than get what you want.

○ *Whom* you do it with.

For example, I sometimes agree to attend events without doing any research. I want to help and often say 'yes' without knowing what I am really getting myself into and then I get there and it's really not my thing or, worse still, I find myself in a room with 10 people when 100 were promised and in order to be there I have turned down an event I would have loved to have done! But back to you...

On the left-hand side of your piece of paper, write down what you actually want to do, for example, 'When I am asked to attend an event, I want to take 15 minutes just to think about dates, times, places and what else is likely to be going on that week,' and along the bottom give yourself an affirmation to remind you. An affirmation is a small sentence you can say to yourself over and over again until you get the message. It's advertising a better you, so rather than listening to a jingle advertising a new face cream, why not listen to your own jingle advertising a new life?

Something like this works: 'I will stop and think before committing.' You may have guessed that's one I should use myself. And maybe I should go with this one too: 'I will listen to my own advice more often!'

It all sounds very simple, but the process of getting your thoughts out of your head and onto paper will push you into remembering them and help when you're put into one of those situations again.

Try it – you may find you buy yourself some more time to spend on all those things you want to do but don't have enough space for because you're doing too much for everyone else.

Polarity

Black and white, positive and negative, hot and cold, sweet and sour – do they work with or against each other? Truth is, they can do both and it's knowing how to put them together that makes the difference. What part of yourself don't you like and what part are you happy to show to the world? And if you don't like something, does it need changing or embracing as part of who you are? Can it serve you in some way? Without my years feeling lost in a world that seemed pointless, how would I have found my way to some meaning?

Knowing the truth of who you are means looking at your positive and negative, your sweet and sour.

I know I can be reclusive, for example, I know I can cut myself off from people at the flick of a phone being switched off and I know I can take to my bed occasionally because frankly I have had enough – but I admit to it. In fact I embrace it – there are times when shutting myself away is the only way I have of balancing out what I have to do versus what I want to do. Having time to myself strengthens the side of me that wants to get out there and help others be all that they can be.

So what do you do? You may speak up when it's inappropriate, you may say things you don't mean just to get a reaction or you may even tell a mate they look lovely when they look a right minger, but whatever you do, you do it for a reason, and that reason is usually the sweet to your sour. Speaking up inappropriately, for instance, is a way of breaking a stalemate, saying things you don't mean to get a reaction creates movement and change, and telling your mate they look lovely when they really don't means you want to pull and they are far too attractive, so any help you can get is a good thing!

Now take a deep breath and admit to whatever you do that isn't your brightest attribute. Then see why you do it. And now, how about simply saying you need to move things on, create change or tell your mate they are fabulous but could they at least think about leaving some fairy dust for you?

Stopping and looking at whatever you do, sweet or sour, out of habit, routine or just because that's how you think things are done is a good thing. It opens your eyes to who you are in all your glory – yes, even including your so-called faults.

Try this visualization to help you along the way:

Get yourself comfortable. Have a nice open posture with your feet firmly planted on the floor and your hands palms up, resting on your legs. Light a candle if you so wish.

Now see yourself outside a house. What kind of house isn't important, just see a house and inside that house know there's your opposite number, your shadow self if you like.

They are waiting for you. They will be happy to see you – they have nothing to fear from you or you from them.

Walk into the house and take your time to look at it as you do so. Just what state of repair is it in? Have you neglected this part of yourself for too long?

Move into the room you know your shadow self is in and see them there. They will look like you but they may be dishevelled, unkempt, with messy hair and tatty clothes.

Ask them what it is that you do and what they think you do it for. Be honest.

They will smile and tell you, this less than shiny side of yourself.

Now ask them how you can incorporate this lesson into your life now. How can what you think of as a weakness become a strength?

They will tell you, and as they do they will transform in front of you, becoming shiny and clean, happy to be a part of who you are.

Leave them in what is now a lovely home, knowing that whatever you do that others don't agree with, it's your way of using the whole of who you are.

Walk away from the house with a smile on your face, ready to embrace the sweet and the sour to make a perfectly balanced dish.

Open your eyes, wiggle your fingers and toes and go and eat something. Chinese perhaps?

Secret: You have no faults, you have opportunities.

✪ ✪ ✪ ✪

So now you know a little more about yourself. Of course that's not all there is to it – your whole *life* is about finding out more about yourself. And there are myriad ways to do it – paranormal, psychic and spiritual.

Ghost of a Chance?

Let's start with the paranormal. No book on psychic secrets would be complete without mentioning traditional haunting, the stuff you see on television and have maybe experienced yourself. Perhaps you have ventured into the world of the paranormal by booking onto one of the many ghost hunts that are available throughout the world. It's a popular pastime, but for me it's the first rung of your spiritual adventure. Some people, of course, bypass it altogether. As I said before, it's all down to what you want to do.

I am still asked to visit places with paranormal activity and I do so not because of the possibility of phenomena but because I know I will meet some lovely people – people who are in fact looking for proof that the human soul continues after death, which is not the same as trying to catch an orb or a low-flying coin or stone. It is an experience not to be missed and it can offer you that first insight into the way the process of seeing happens. Also, certainly when I am involved in an investigation, you get the opportunity to use your intuition.

But this isn't the only way into the world of the paranormal. Many of us are drawn to it when we lose someone close to us.

One of the questions I am asked most is whether a loved one who has passed on is OK. People want to know whether their loved ones just find their way forward or whether someone shows them, and if so, who it is.

When you have such questions and want to find the answers it's natural to go to someone who is trained in communicating with the spirit world, and there are many superb mediums out there. Finding one is the thing. In my view, there's nothing like personal recommendation. That applies whether it's a medium, teacher or a plumber – and, just like finding a plumber, price is no guarantee of a job well done. Some of the best readings I've ever had were free and some of the worst cost me a fortune – so get that recommendation.

But there is another way.

When you look at someone who does something that you consider extraordinary, do you think you could never do that or do you think you could if you took the time and had the inclination? Like speaking a foreign language or kicking a football, we are all capable of speaking to spirit, and of course listening as well, if we only take the time to learn.

When a loved one passes, our thoughts inevitably turn towards what happens next and our mind is full of 'What if...?' and 'How about...?', but is this the right time to pontificate or would it be better used by simply allowing ourselves to do what our spiritual bodies do best and *listen* – listen for the whisper of our loved one saying farewell for now?

My father passed only a few years ago and as he did I experienced an amazing string of events, everything from him tapping on my head to let me know he was there right through to the pain of separation as he crossed, but nothing compared to a few days after his death when I was sitting in the lounge and I heard his voice say, 'Bye bye, son.' Everything he was and all that I can be were in that moment and I would never have heard his words had I been dashing about, asking others to do the listening for me and asking the same questions over and over again.

Now you may think that's easy for me because it's what I do. It's what you do too, actually; the only difference is I have had some training. I firmly believe that when it comes to our own family and those we love, the bond between us is so strong that if any of us listen we will hear them.

If you have others to think of – kids to get to school, a dog needing a walk, for instance – you may already be wondering how you can find that space in your life to hear the voices of your loved ones. The good news is that you're likely to do it automatically – there will be moments when you're washing the dishes, doing the ironing or driving the car when you will lose yourself in the mundane tasks of life and even though you'll still be moving, still doing what you have to do, your mind will be elsewhere. That's when you'll hear, and when you do, you'll shake your head and think you imagined it.

So how can we take that a stage further? How can you be sure that you're not imagining it, that you're as able as anyone else to hear that whisper?

First things first: get the kids to school, walk the dog and find some time for yourself. Very important: switch off the phone. Light a candle, look at the flame and the light it gives off and remember what it looks like...

Now sit in your favourite chair, be comfortable and have your feet firmly planted on the floor and your hands palms up, resting on your legs in a nice open posture.

Now close your eyes and visualize that candle again. In your mind's eye remember what it looks like, and as you look at it see the light getting brighter and brighter, moving round you until you are completely surrounded by it. Imagine that you're in the middle of that powerful protective white light.

As you look around the light you will see that it appears to pulsate, to vibrate, and as it does it's changing your vibration. You feel lighter and happier, you feel the joy of this place and the love that surrounds you.

Ahead of you there's a chair – any kind of chair you like, just let one appear. See yourself moving towards it and taking your seat. Feel comfortable.

Look up now and you will see a doorway. It seems to be built into the light in some way, and as you look at it, the door opens and from an even brighter light comes ... who?

Sometimes a guide may appear, but as you're in the world of astral beings it's more likely to be someone who has passed that wishes to communicate with you. Have your conversation and above all go with the moment, enjoy this link.

When you are both ready, see the person move back through the door and let it close behind them. Be happy in the knowledge that they are safe and well.

Now leave your chair and walk back to where you first entered the light.

Pause a while and allow the light to once more raise your vibration. Allow yourself to feel loved and protected.

When you're ready, see the light reduce in size, see it return to the size of your candle and then open your eyes and focus on the real candle.

Again when you're ready, stand up and get that kettle on, dunk a biscuit or two and write down your experience.

So what's the secret here? We are all made of spirit, it's our natural place in the universe, so you are always connected to those you love, it's just that sometimes a little effort is required to remind you of it.

✪ ✪ ✪ ✪

But what if it's where you live that is giving you some food for thought?

Cox's Mill Inn

I was invited to a lovely hotel at the foot of Cheddar Gorge, not to do a paranormal investigation in the usual way but to help the owners understand just what was going on, and what was refreshing about Cox's Mill was they didn't want any attempt made to cleanse the place, they simply wanted to know who was there and why. They wanted to live among their ghosts.

The mill is an interesting building and sits right on the end of a weir. In fact, one of the bedrooms has a balcony that looks over the millpond, which is of course elevated to feed the water wheel. This bedroom was to be the centre of our investigation.

Looking around the mill for the first time, I realized it was clearly much older in some places than others. It didn't feel threatening in any way and as the owner showed me round I was aware of astral activity, but nothing right in my face!

When you enter a building that is reputed to be haunted it's best to do so with no preconceptions and to take each event as it comes, but above all you must trust your intuition and listen to it! So what little secret can I give you to help?

Switching on and off is something you will hear sensitives talk about all the time. Switching on is a way of heightening your awareness so you can feel paranormal activity around you. It seems to me there are many ways to do it and it all depends on how you're trained. Here's something I do with groups when I go on an investigation:

Get everyone to stand in a circle (yes, even the hard-faced sceptics, in fact them especially), hold hands and get cosy. Holding hands helps with the energy movement you're about to do but also takes away the possibility that the tickle you feel on your nose is your mate goofing about rather than anything from beyond the veil!

Now ask everyone to close their eyes.

See above your head a brilliant white light. Really see it shining as brightly as you can, and when you think it's really bright, turn up the brightness another notch.

Now see this light move down into your crown and down the left-hand side of your head and face. See it move down your shoulders and arms and then into your left hand.

Now feel the energy from the person on your right in your right hand and let it work its way up your arm, into your shoulder, along the right-hand side of your face and into the ball of light at the top of your head.

Now there's white light all the way round the circle. This is a light of protection as well as attraction and can be seen by the astral worlds.

Say a protection prayer. I say the Qabalistic prayer, but you can use anything you want as long as you stick to it – power is built with use.

For those of you who want to try the Qabalistic prayer, it is the last part of the Lord's Prayer in Hebrew: 'As above, so below, the power and the glory, for ever and ever, amen.' We say, 'Ateh, Malkuth, Ve Geburha, Ve Gedula, Le Olam, Amen.' Phonetically, that's 'Ah-tay, Mal-kuth [some say "Mal coot" here, that's fine too, it's a pronunciation thing, just go with how you've been taught], Vay Gay-boora, Vay Gay-doo-lah, Lay Oo-lam, Amen.'

When doing this, put the sign of the cross on yourself with your right hand, starting at your head for 'Ateh' and moving to your groin for 'Malkuth', your right shoulder for 'Ve Geburah' and your left for 'Ve Gedulah' and then bringing both your hands together as if praying for 'Le Olam' and bowing as you say 'Amen.'

When you say it, make sure you vibrate it, almost sing it, and don't be shy, belt it out!

Now see another white light, a light coming from your heart area, your heart chakra.

Let everyone's heart chakra light go out into the middle of the circle like the spokes in a wheel, and as they meet, a ball of light is created.

Make this ball of light large enough to almost fill the centre of the circle. See it as sparkling white light.

Concentrate on the ball and let it act as a movie screen, showing you events from the building you're investigating. These are likely to be residual energy, in other words records from the past showing you the building's true history. Some of you may see one part of its history while others will link in with individuals who once lived there or maybe get a sensation of an incident that happened there, but remember it may not always be what the building is famous for, so don't go by the guidebook. In fact, if your group is getting nothing but guidebook stuff you may need to take a little break and have a little word! The key is to get people to speak up. The divination process is lost when everyone goes away wondering whether what they saw was real or not, and all it takes is for someone to say what you know you're seeing to prove it to you.

So let the images form, and as they do, tell others what you are seeing. You may find they are seeing the same thing!

When you're ready, see the white light lift upwards. Send that ball of light out into the universe to be used for positive events. Send it up and out into the night sky with love.

Now see your own lights return to the ball above your head and send that too out into the universe.

Wiggle your fingers and your toes and bring your consciousness back into the room.

Compare notes and see how each of you felt during this visualization.

Take a break. Have some tea and cake.

TROUBLE AT T'MILL

So what was going on at the mill? It was time to switch on, tune in and get out there.

In the bar area there was a blustery energy behind the serving counter, an energy that was in a hurry and presented as a highwayman complete with tricorn hat and black cloak – how very exciting! He moved fast and there had been reports of things falling off the counter and people sensing someone moving past them. He was also moving where there would have been a wall originally, going around the back of the building, no doubt.

Upstairs there was a sensation of people rushing past me in a panic. At first I thought they were escaping a fire, but I was informed there hadn't been a fire there. Still, they were in a panic and later I found out why.

For now it was into another room where an older woman showed herself. There was a connection to a child – was she looking for this child or was she protecting it? She was a strong presence and I was told others had seen her and reported that she did indeed seem to be looking for someone or something. She sometimes woke guests up – nice, when all you want is a good night's sleep!

In room 11 there was a strong male energy. A man made himself known – severe in approach, wearing lots of black and sporting a top hat. He put his fingers to his lips in a gesture that told me he wanted silence. He also seemed to be looking for his family. This was, by coincidence (or maybe not), a family room. Once, when a young family was staying there, the mother had woken up in the night to see this man standing at the bottom of her bed – confirmation for the owner that he was around, I suspect.

Next it was the bedroom overlooking the weir. It had a four-poster bed in it and a great view over the mill-pond, but it felt disjointed, unhappy, though not so that you couldn't bear it. The woman I'd seen earlier seemed to be present, as was another energy. This was definitely the busiest room in the hotel.

I did a lone vigil, calling out and attempting to contact whoever was in the room, but all I got was a woman coming into the room. I saw her do it again and again, but I never saw her leave. She wasn't communicating, certainly not with me, she was just coming in with a panicky look on her face and that was it, she faded and then she did it all again.

With longer at the mill, I am sure I would have witnessed more paranormal activity and been able to learn more about what had happened there, but I only had a couple of hours before heading home, so I asked the owners what the story was.

It turned out that the bedroom overlooking the millpond had been the scene of a great tragedy. The picture I was seeing was that of a former owner who had come into the room to find her husband having an affair with another woman. So distraught was she at the sight that she ran to the balcony and threw herself into the millpond, where she drowned. Here, then, was the reason for the panic, as everyone ran out of the building to get to the pond to rescue her – all too late.

Was the man in black her husband? Why was he looking for his family? Who was the older woman I'd seen and where was the child she was looking for? That's for future investigation.

Reviewing the Situation

It's always a good thing to ask those who live among such activity what they want done about it. It's their house, after all. Remember, though, that even if they would like whatever is there to move on, it's not always possible for a sensitive to do it. A spirit has free will, too, so it's sometimes a case of following Tony Ainsworth's advice as described later in this book.

In this case the owners were happy to live with the other residents. I think they were right, as they weren't causing any problems and were in fact a way of understanding the link between this world and others, so all that was left was to explain that simply acknowledging them when they pulled the plug out of the Hoover or knocked over a glass or two was akin to welcoming an old friend back!

Ethics and Ghost Hunting

I am often asked how ghost hunting should be done. There are no formal rules and all I can offer are my own principles, which aren't meant as a judgement on the methods of others but are based on hundreds of investigations of my own:

O   Don't gatecrash a location, get permission first, and most definitely never trespass on what could be dangerous property.

○ Make sure you have a sensitive with you that you trust and have some technical or rational balance – don't assume that everything that happens is paranormal.

○ Orbs are often cited as the first manifestation of spiritual life, but I am not convinced. They're usually dust, and if they're not dust, they're possibly an insect or moisture on the camera. If they *are* evidence of spiritual life, it's likely they are just the tail end of astral light as the energy moves around, and that's more impressive seen with your own eyes rather than digital cameras, which have a tendency to produce the orb effect with dust, insects and moisture!

○ The best piece of equipment is your intuition. Go with it and question what you get after the event rather than when you're there in the midst of it.

○ Laughter helps with energy – do plenty of it.

○ Fear helps with awareness – get scared and turn your animal instincts up.

○ If you feel ill, get out of there.

○ Sitting in silence works as well as yakking away.

○ Visualization and meditation can help you get 'pictures'.

○ Disturb nothing and take nothing away with you, particularly not the Rembrandt.

○ Know yourself and know what your 'tell' is, i.e. what happens to you when you feel astrals walking around you. For me it's a sensation of spiders' webs falling on my face or a tingling all over. Sometimes I feel a tap on my head. Other people report one hand feeling hot, their ears being pulled, or even, as one person told me, that they have the feeling they are being watched and can see lots of eyes looking at them – yes, that would certainly make me feel as if I was being watched! The point is, who cares what it is? If you get a vision of Elvis, it's your tell, so use it!

○ When dealing with 'otherworldly' visitors, there's no need to channel, scream, shout or use language best 'left to roughty toughty sailors. Just be courteous and act with some humanity.

Really, there's no magic formula. Remember most people see things when they are carrying out mundane tasks like washing up, cleaning the floors or just waiting for another group of tourists to stop gawping at the third duke's suit of armour.

Encountering the local astral world in this way is enough for some people, as already mentioned, but if you want to move beyond things that go bump in the night you will need to bump yourself up a level to talk to guides and helpers.

Let's start with elementals.

Chapter 2

It's Elemental, Dear Frankie

t's not every day you get a telephone call asking you to visit a childhood hero's home, but that's what happened. Apparently there were problems at Wavering Down, the home of British comedy legend Frankie Howerd, and they wanted to know what was going on.

Frankie had passed in 1992 and of course the first thing that went through my mind was that he might be unhappy about something or simply have returned to visit a place I assumed he loved – pretty obvious, I agree, but it's been my experience that the simplest explanations are usually the right ones. But how wrong was I proved!

But back to the story as it unfolded. A date was set and I found myself on the road to Wavering

Down, Frankie's home in a little village at the foot of the Mendip Hills. Greeting me at the door was Chris Byrne, a friend of Frankie's and chairman of the Frankie Howerd OBE Trust.

As we entered the house, still decorated for Christmas in late January due to upcoming parties for charity, I was aware of a heaviness, a distinct change in atmosphere.

Usually on entering premises like this I immediately get an impression of who is around me, I start to tingle and my subconscious mind is out there trying to find anyone who may want to chat from the spiritual worlds, but this time nothing came back. I was still aware of the heaviness in the air but thought it best to give things time to settle around me. I was, after all, in Frankie's house and excited at the prospect of having a good old look around.

Chris explained what he had been feeling in the house very briefly, as too much information before an investigation can be off-putting and I would advise anyone attempting to sense energies in a place to go in with an open mind rather than a head full of other people's opinions. Chris also told me about Frankie's death and showed me some wonderful things that he had been given by some amazing stars such as Richard Burton, Elizabeth Taylor and Zsa Zsa Gabor. He was a true comedy legend, but it was no secret that he was also a nervous man and no doubt difficult to live with at times. I wondered what effect that would have had on his own space.

We all give off an energy, a force that's transmitted through our aura, that part of us that seems to go before us, to warn others of our mood and perhaps that part of us that's left behind when we have exited the room, or in this case the human body. Could I sense Frankie? Was that who or what I was feeling as Chris showed me Frankie's favourite chair, which he took with him every time he had to be filmed giving an interview – an armchair, nothing too portable! – and the portrait commissioned for him by Queen Elizabeth the Queen Mother?

If objects give off an aura from their owners, I was at a Hollywood gala, what with the swords used by Burton and Taylor in *Cleopatra* being handed to me, as well as many incredible items that were tributes to Frankie from those in his business who loved him and his work.

But still there was that feeling of being watched.

Chris told me he couldn't sleep upstairs in the house, he wasn't comfortable there and felt as if he wasn't welcome. Clearly, then, that was where I had to go next.

Walking along the corridor towards the staircase I was aware of a feeling of anticipation in the air, of stepping ever closer to the lair of something that knew you would come to it, that had no need to find you as you would inevitably be drawn to it.

Climbing the stairs, I was conscious of Chris becoming more nervous and to be honest I half-expected Frankie to pop up and ask me to leave, but there was no sign of him other than the copious numbers of giant photographs of him in various comic guises and poses looking down at me from the walls. However, there was something else waiting for me.

It was like walking into a brick wall – the energy almost stopped me at the top of the stairs and I had to push myself on and through it. Then there it was: a great black energy mass in the form of a large dog, red-eyed and glaring at me. It was a scary sight, but I knew it couldn't harm me – it wasn't physical and no matter how much it threatened me it couldn't throw me down the stairs or bite me. It couldn't even lick me if it felt like it. It might have chosen to appear as a dog in order to scare me, but I knew it was in fact a mass of energy masquerading as man's best friend!

I asked Chris and friends to go back downstairs to the kitchen, where I explained what I had found.

The energy and how it worked were confirmed by Chris, as he himself had thought he had seen a dog or large black shape upstairs.

The problem was elemental. What does that mean? Bear with me! If there are four elemental forces in the world, one of Air, one of Fire, one of Water and one of Earth, it's clear they should be in balance to make for a perfect energetic set-up. Perfection isn't something that happens in life, though, not without effort – we all have to work at it and sometimes we get it wrong. This situation was way out of balance.

Here Earth energy had taken over – dense energy was pulling everything down. The Earth was negating the Fire, Air and Water that should have kept the house lighter and brighter. Don't believe me? Shut your windows, put out all of your candles, remove your plants and flowers and shut the curtains – does that make your home feel less balanced?

Chris admitted he only lit a candle on Frankie's birthday and at Easter and Christmas. Every window in the house was closed and never opened, there were no real plants or flowers there and no animals living in the house – there was just the house itself, the energy of Frankie and a great big well-fed stormy Earth elemental, an amalgamation of it all helped along by the lack of movement in the house.

Things had been the same for years – even the coat hanging on the banister was Frankie's. It was as if he had never left, which was of course the idea behind leaving it there.

So, what to do?

Everyone gathered in the kitchen and it was up to me to deal with the problem. I walked upstairs on my own to confront Fido. He was waiting for me, putting on quite a show, growing in size to encompass me and making the air thick with his presence and my body feel under pressure, as if I were a deep-sea diver, but I settled myself calmly and took a seat right in the midst of his space.

I was mindful of the fact that I was in someone's home, someone I admired and respected, and there really was no need to get anyone else involved or to make a big fuss channelling this, chanting that or screaming about the place making everyone nervous. There never is. Dramas can make things tougher to deal with; shows of exaggerated terror produce energy of their own and end up feeding rather than starving energy such as this.

It's actually dangerous to offer more food to an already out-of-control energy, dangerous not because it will bite you or eat you up, but it could bring about an imbalance in you, leading to moods, an unhappy home and eventually what you may think of as life trials like a break-up in a relationship, duplicity with partners, children being very difficult – all sorts of things. We are all energy and everything around us is energy and it's a case of cause and effect. Get that and you get smart!

So Fido and I simply had a chat. This wasn't his home, it belonged to someone else. It wasn't his place to use so much energy and to get territorial about it, so here was the deal: he could stay, but in a much reduced state. His energy was as important as that of Air, Fire and Water, but not any more so. I visualized him shrinking, becoming more of a lapdog than a guard dog, and firmly reminded him of his place.

Chris was invited to go back upstairs on his own and when he returned he said he had a feeling the dog was saying, 'Spoilsport!' Good. I had intended to spoil its sport and to this day things are calmer in the house.

But Chris must also play his part. Fire, Air and Water have to be brought into the house and a balance struck. Getting those windows open, introducing fresh flowers and lighting a few candles may not seem like much, but that's the point – it shouldn't be an effort to introduce the balancing effects of the elements in your home.

It was time to say goodbye to Frankie's house and I was glad to be leaving it brighter than when I had arrived and delighted that my hero's home would be happier for it.

The Elements and You

We all have the elements in our lives – in fact, we are all made up of all of them. They combine within us, but often one will predominate. Which element are you? Do you have the burning passion of Fire, the stubbornness of Earth, the lightness of Air or the emotional depths of Water? Truth is, you have all four, but recognizing which is dominant and when could help you sort out some issues in your life – and much more quickly than you might think. So how do you know which is which and how to recognize them in yourself?

Astrology

Astrology can help. Right from the off, your Sun sign, that's your star sign, gives you a clue. Gemini, Libra and Aquarius are Air signs, Aries, Leo and Sagittarius are Fire signs, Cancer, Scorpio and Pisces are Water signs, and finally Taurus, Virgo and Capricorn are Earth signs. Of course, there is much more to it when you think about your Moon sign, your rising sign, where Pluto is in your chart and so on, but your Sun sign is a good starting-point.

But remember how you *feel* is just as valid. Which element are you most drawn to? And what does it mean?

AIR
If you're an Air sign or attracted to Air, you're likely to be the talkative sort, the kind who likes to chat, but fairly superficially – you might not dig as deep as you might! You're likely to be here, there and back again before you know it and then off again... Light and frothy, funny and social – yes, that's all fine, but sometimes you may need to take things a little more seriously.

FIRE
With Fire to the fore, you're passionate and argumentative, creative and ready to give anything a go, but sometimes of course that could turn out to be a little reckless. You're probably the sporty type, either playing or watching, and you're difficult to keep in one place for too long, as your natural instinct is to get up and go. So just go and do something, will you?!

WATER
Watery individuals are emotional souls, whether they express that or keep it in, whether they cry at

adverts on TV or save it until they curl up in a ball at the end of the day with heartfelt emotions, fighting to make sense of what's going on in their world. This is a sensitive element; it carries the psychic intuitive gene and it makes its users sensitive to the world around them.

EARTH
The great beasts of the elemental kingdoms symbolize the Earth sign! That's beasts of burden as well as forces that can move mountains. These are the builders and architects of the systems and routines that keep everything in its place and a place for everything. This can sometimes result in stubbornness, though, being unable to budge and unable to get out of that rut.

Which One Are You?
Time to meditate, so get yourself comfortable and think about how full your tummy is, how loose your clothing is and just how lovely it is to switch those telephones off!

Take a deep breath, let it out, and as you do, let all that tension go, just let it go. Let your shoulders relax and breathe deeply. Keep that rhythm going.

Now imagine you're in a forest. Let it build around you and let it fill your senses. See it, hear it, smell it, taste it and touch it.

In this forest you will see a path, a path that you feel compelled to follow, and as you do you're aware that this is a new route for you, a new way through your forest, one you're excited to walk.

It takes you deeper into the forest, deeper and deeper and down a small slope, into a lush forest glade surrounded by trees.

Sit there on the lush grass, in fact lie down and feel the element of Earth all around you, surrounding you, seducing you with the comfort of its smells and sounds.

In the distance, hear a bell ring.

Passing by is a procession of the elementals, a magnificent spectacle and one you know you're privileged to see. Say nothing, just watch.

First the sylphs of Air appear, buzzing around with brightly coloured light trailing in their wake – the embodiment of fast-paced chatter and quick-thinking minds.

As they pass, the salamanders of Fire take their place – sparks of light burning brightly, flaring up and then fading away, the embodiment of a bright idea that must be seized or lost forever.

Now it's the turn of the undines, the sparkle of water on the crest of a wave and the slow relaxing swell of the sea as it cradles and nurtures your very existence, the embodiment of your tears, the ebb and flow of your emotions.

Finally the gnomes of Earth appear and matter-of-factly stomp through, tidying up and repairing the Earth they love so dearly. They have a routine, they have a system, and they embody the need for it in our own lives.

You find yourself still lying on the grass. Did you dream it all?

Sit up and look around you. There's no sign of any elementals, but you know they were there. You know they are there.

Which elemental were you most drawn to? Which one's song can you still hear in your heart?

Now make your way out of the clearing and into the forest, back along your path.

Wander along that path until it begins to fade and you return to your normal surroundings.

Take a deep breath, let it go and open your eyes.

Kettle on, biscuits out.

As usual, write up your experience. Remember, keeping a record of your visualizations is a great way to ground them, to help you recall them and to look back and see how far you have come!

Ask yourself which element you were drawn to and which one you really felt nothing for at all.

So now you have a better idea of how you feel about the elements, what next?

Working with the Elements

Thomas was a friend of mine who would wake up angry. He knew he wasn't angry at anything or anyone in particular, just angry. It didn't happen all the time – more often than not he was a friendly sort, a kind and warm-hearted individual – but he was an Aries with his Moon in Aries and several other planets in the Fire signs, so he was over-polarized with the energy of the salamanders and sometimes it would take very little to raise his temperature.

Initially he was sceptical, a good thing to be, but he was also open. I suggested that when he felt that way the first thing he should do was to look to see if it was due to anything directly affecting his life. Was it a person or a situation that had him feeling frustrated and looking for a fight? If it was, he should go and sort it out. If it wasn't, was it something on a grander scale? Was it an elemental balance that was out of sorts? If he felt it was, I suggested he took himself to the beach, regardless of the weather, to walk along the seafront with the wind in his face and the water beside him and to pick up stones and attach his anger to them and throw them into the sea to be cleansed and taken from him. I suggested he visualized his anger as boiling red, saw the rock in his hand turning red and then cast it into that cleansing ocean.

He of course thought I was bonkers – nothing new – but he tried it the next time he felt the frustration rising in him. Of course it worked, why else would I be telling you it in this book, I'm hardly going to put it in if it hadn't now, am I?! Now he uses it not only when he can't attach an earthly problem to the situation but even when he can. It's not always the beach either – Tom has now taken to the forest and added mountain biking to his list of interests, a tough sport for all that Fire to be absorbed by. He's much calmer now – funny, that!

Whilst no single attribute of any of the elements is a bad thing, over-polarizing may not be the best idea. If you're a fiery sort, are you perhaps *too* fiery? Do you rush into things when a better way of dealing with them would be to look at them with the practicality that Earth could bring or the logic that Air would add to the proceedings? Or do you perhaps need to have Water poured on the situation in the form of true emotions to calm everything down?

Here are a few tips if you think you're over-enthusiastic with one particular element:

○   *Air:* If you chatter when you ought to sit back and ponder, or you can't sit still long enough to take things seriously, you may have too much Air in your make-up.

To calm it down, particularly when you need to be more practical, try introducing some Earth. Make sure you write things down, thereby earthing your ideas and making them tangible rather than leaving them floating around in the ether unused or, worse still, available for others to pinch! Get a list and check it twice. Also, put some representatives of the element Earth in your life: add plants to your environment, eat organic well-sourced food or put some sea salt in your bath. It may not sound like much, but you're actively suggesting to yourself that you calm down, pay attention and get things done rather than just talk about them.

Fire could also be introduced to get you moving. The colours of flame in your clothing or your décor could motivate you, and remember to light a candle daily – though don't leave it unattended, of course! Fire warms and comforts us, but it also makes us feel enthusiastic enough to take action.

○ *Fire:* If you're first up, ready to go without thinking about the consequences and in danger of making a real pig's ear of the whole thing, you may have too much Fire in you. And the risks of over-polarization count double when Fire is the element in question. The danger is you botch the whole deal, rush in where angels fear to tread and end up dealing with things you really had no need to go near in the first place.

Of course, Earth is going to help you – it quells those flames, but don't add so much it puts them out. That's not the point at all. What you need is to confine them, which will help you to direct the fire where you need it most. Earth will bring structure and practical solutions and it will add safety to the proceedings. So bring plants into your home, get out and do some gardening, and if you're really brave, why not put your fiery nature to good use and jump out of an aeroplane for charity – with a parachute, of course!

Air can also help you find support for your plans, but if using Air please don't add too much or you could end up with an explosion of ideas that are destructive rather than constructive, as you just won't know which one to tackle first!

Water may seem like the obvious choice to put out too much Fire, but will it bring balance or take over completely? Think before going for the obvious – too much emotion would slow you down and eventually end up dampening that wonderful spirit of Fire. Work with, not to the detriment of, your strengths.

○ *Water:* Reaching for the handkerchief before the opening titles of *Who Will Love My Children?* is a natural thing, but if you're doing it for *The Simpsons* you may have too much Water in your chart – that or an empathy with Marge (why do you think her hair is blue?). Water is the element that has your boss complaining you're too emotionally involved or your family suggesting you let things go rather than put in an ending that's unlikely to happen! 'I can't help it!' you may cry. Truth is, you can. You can recognize it, you can feel it, in fact we should all feel it, but what you do with all this emotion is the point.

Bring in some Air, which makes bubbles, and we all know that bubbles add lightness. How do you do it? You have conversations about how you feel, you let people know why you're feeling that way, you listen to what they have to say to that and you let it sink in – that is, you allow yourself to rationalize what you feel! Air can of course also be added by opening the windows and getting out more. That's a good one – get those elements around you and have Mother Nature restore your natural balance.

Good old Earth is also once more high on the list of remedies – organizational skills will put plans into action and if you have had those conversations you will know where you're going, leaving little room for emotional tidal waves to move in.

○ *Earth:* Hard to budge, stubborn and set in your ways, a little bit of a jobsworth and not given to spontaneity? It's not easy being practical all of the time, but there are benefits when playing the long, slow game. Still, life is sometimes about quick thinking and opportunities that won't hang around, so add some Air, Fire and of course some Water. Aerate earth and you get better soil in which to grow things; add some water and some warm sunshine and you have perfect conditions for growth.

Earth is the element that in my humble opinion can calm and control all others. It stands to reason therefore that it needs the others to make itself stable. Too much Earth means inaction, so add deadlines to your life, put in some Fire by challenging yourself physically, add Air by doing the same mentally and open the floodgates to Water by admitting to how you feel rather than hiding behind the dam of stubbornness. To help you remember your need for the elements to be in balance, have representations of them around your home, with Air in the east, Fire in the west, Water in the south and Earth in the north.

The elements are the building blocks of the universe, and of all the secrets you will receive in this book, this is one of the greatest. If you learn to understand and work with the elements you will begin to create peace and harmony in your life as well as welcoming in a force that will open up your future and make all things seem possible.

If you use Tarot cards, think about the suits, think about Swords, Wands, Cups and Discs and what they represent, and you will see they correspond to Air, Fire, Water and Earth. All are linked – all you have to do is find the pathways and you will uncover your own secrets, your own way of understanding your inner self.

To recap:

○ Elementals are forces of Air, Fire, Water and Earth.

○ We are all made up of all four elements:

Air represents the mind, conscious thoughts and ideas.

Fire is all about passion, action and creativity.

Water is our emotions and our nurturing nature.

Earth represents our practical side. It's a building block.

○ If we can balance these elements in ourselves, our lives will be more balanced.

○ Tarot cards display the elements in their suits.

Do the meditation, if you haven't already, and see which of the elementals you want to dance with and which you wish would just hurry up and get past you! The ones you don't care for much say just as much about you as those you want to get up and dance with.

Now write down how you feel, what you think about elementals and elements and just what you can do to restore and keep your balance. Are you more Water than Fire? Are you more Earth than Air?

When you become more comfortable with the idea, why not find some music that is very Airy in its nature, or a sparkling little number that reminds you of Water, or a hot Latin beat that says, 'Fire, Fire, Fire,' or maybe a ploddy, practical Earthy tune to encourage more practicality in your life?

Colours, archangels, sounds, smells and sights of the natural world all have an association with an element. Take them and make them your own. Creativity will bring the elementals alive in your life and once they are, there's no end of surprises ahead of you.

There's much more on elements on
www.orderofthewhitelion.com.

✿ ✿ ✿ ✿

But what happens if you encounter something that
you don't feel is elemental? What if you think it's
something less than heaven sent?

Chapter 3

Psychic Challenge

Martin and his lovely wife had just moved into a new house. A happy home and a more loving couple you would be hard pushed to find. But after a little while Martin started to hear his name being called. He thought it was his wife calling, but it wasn't her. Then he began to feel someone close to him. And the occasional object moving around the house wasn't exactly making either of them feel very comfortable and was even making them argue, something they had never done before.

As well as their day jobs, both Martin and his wife were paranormal investigators with a very successful group in the south. They loved to go ghost hunting at weekends and they enjoyed helping others. I have to say both were very good at what they did and clearly, to my mind, their interest was activating their own abilities, which is often the case. It's similar to working in another country – you may be there to lay bricks but you're going to pick up the language along the way. Still, that's not what Martin thought was going on.

'Until Death Do Us Part'

Martin was convinced he had been 'sent' an energy, sent some bad luck or some sort of entity to make his life difficult, and he thought he knew where it had come from – an ex. So he imagined his home surrounded by a mirror ball, which is a great technique for reflecting and sending back negative energy. He was also right to remember that ill will comes back tenfold on those who think they have some sort of right to interfere in the lives of others.

But it didn't work.

Martin asked me to visit the house and when I walked in I was honest and said I felt nothing, nothing at all. I talked to both him and his wife and it seemed to me that whatever or whoever it was that had affected the house they had dealt with it successfully and it had gone, but I was concerned that they were bringing negative energy back for a whole other reason.

I don't believe energies come home with you – what's so exciting in our lives that they just want to be a part of? – and if you use psychic protection before you work, as described earlier, that goes double, but too much dwelling in the darkness without taking steps to ground yourself in the light could be a problem. Let me explain.

A Balancing Act

If your balance between Earth, Air, Fire and Water is out of the window you already know it has to be restored, but what if you're thinking, living and breathing the paranormal world all the time? Could you become so obsessed by it that every noise becomes a voice or every natural occurrence becomes supernatural?

My advice, if you ever feel this is happening to you, is to allow yourself to watch something that isn't of this genre on telly more often than you do, to make sure you have a rational approach to all such events and to remember your *psychic* self, your psyche, what's affecting your mind and your thought patterns.

Martin had taken control by putting something in place he believed in, which told his mind and his body that it was being sorted – a great psychic technique. After that he also had a natural break from all things paranormal due to work commitments abroad and he started reading some very interesting books that took him out of the paranormal, into the psychic and through to the spiritual arena. Knowledge from a different viewpoint brought him out of his mindset, and is still doing so to this day, and as his vibration increases so does that of the space around him. He is a truly lovely soul and has a deep compassion for people that will, I am sure, be better served on his new path.

Psychic Housekeeping

So, what can you do to keep your psychic self tidy?

First of all, are you sure you have one? I know you have and I know you think you have, but how do you prove it? Can your mind truly pick up on ideas and scenarios around you? And if it can, what about affecting that web and putting your will and your intention out there? Can you do that too?

The secret is of course rule number one, which is: *harm none.* If you're doing any kind of work where others are involved, you must do so with the highest of intention and perhaps some wish for proof! I hold no court with those who seek to do harm or interfere with people's paths and I know there are higher powers that re-address that balance in time.

So, with that secret in mind, would you like to experiment with your psychic powers? Try this and see what happens:

Make yourself comfortable and switch off that phone!

Take some deep breaths in and out, and as you breathe out, let all your tensions and anxieties go.

Now see a large white ball of light in front of you. Make it larger and larger until it looks like a giant screen.

On that screen see an event in your future. See what you're doing and how well you're doing it. Date it, if you like. I do that by seeing a calendar in the corner.

Now reinforce how well you're doing and play the whole video again to make sure your subconscious gets that message!

Next see the whole picture surrounded in pink light – pink, the colour of love and good intent.

To send it out into the universe, imagine breathing in that pink light, but in through your crown, the top of your head, and out through your heart chakra, the energy point that transmits and receives love.

Now let that pink bubble float off into the universe to program success!

Open your eyes, wiggle your toes and your fingers and have some tea and cake.

Give it a go – you may be very pleasantly surprised with the results, I have done this around the world with people and I love it when they e-mail me to tell me that their brother actually managed to empty the dishwasher or their husband found the Hoover!

The more serious and practical side is of course the thought that you could use this to remind yourself that you can have what you want in life and attract it to you. Cosmic ordering is simply that: work out what you want, see it coming to you, see it coming to you again and never lose sight of it.

Hot Seat

Your aura – remember, that light that surrounds you and is sometimes referred to as your energy – isn't just made up of pretty colours and sparkly lights, it also contains your emotions. It can transfer what's going on with you emotionally into pictures and symbols which can be read by those who take the time and whom you allow in. You can, in turn, read the emotions of other people in the same way. It's another way of using your psychic skills without tools such as the Tarot. (Of course, when the Tarot is being used, most readers are reading your aura, whether you or they know it or not!)

Extending this a little more, try this very easy way to start to use your psychic senses:

Get a friend to sit opposite you and ask them to visualize a giant light around them, to make it as bright as they can and to see themselves inside that bubble.

Now ask them to see pictures and symbols in the light, to put in a few if they want, but not to tell you what they are seeing.

Give them time to do it.

When they have finished, ask them to stand up.

Now make your way to their chair.

Sit in the chair and see yourself walking into the energy that is there. What can you see, what pictures come to you?

Talk it out, let your friend know what you are seeing.

How did you do?

Remember to write down what you saw and of course to have some tea and ... let's make it biscuits this time.

This exercise is to show you that you are as capable as anyone else of using your birthright: your psychic self.

The psychic challenge is to find what works for you. Remember it doesn't matter which method you use as long as you get the results you want. But remember too that all the ways of working are there to help others as well as you...

Half-hearted Harriet

Part of your spiritual and psychic growth may involve undertaking things that don't make you feel very comfortable. By that I am not talking about anything that goes against your beliefs or your morals – those things are very simply dealt with by walking away, and please be quick about it – what I am talking about are things like accepting that energy can be moved by sound, therefore if you make more sound, surely energy will be moved faster – yes, it's the 'Why are you chanting and do I have to join in?' question!

You don't have to do anything you don't want to do, however there will be times when you can see the value of what's being discussed and you really owe it to yourself to give it a go. And if you're going to give it a go, you give it a go! Better to be a give-it-a-go Jo than a half-hearted Harriet. Belt it out, belt out your chant or your vibration as loud as you can. Make it loud enough to blow the froth off your mate's cappuccino from three tables away!

The psychic secret is to give it your all. Because without giving it your all, how do you know it works?

Belief – Take your Pipe and Stick It

I am often asked when I first knew I was psychic. It's like being asked, 'When did you first know you were Scottish?' – it's always been there. Of course that doesn't mean I didn't have times when I wondered how I dared assume such a thing or even a day or three when I thought, 'What a load of old rubbish this psychic malarkey is.' Of course I did and still do. I see healthy scepticism as a very important part of what I do and I question all the time; blind faith is no faith. Those who tout absolute belief without question are as tough to deal with as those who tout absolute lack of belief. They are in the same camp as far as I am concerned.

Testing your beliefs is therefore allowed. This is a personal thing. I've heard stories of floating carpets and fully manifest beings wandering around popping the kettle on and practically running around with the Hoover, but I haven't seen them. On the other hand, I've had sceptics tell me that everything I've seen is just my imagination and my brain playing tricks, but still I see magic every day in the world.

What I do know is the answers are always going to be personal, and that's your starting point, my fellow seeker. If what you sense rings true with you, then that's enough. If you can't quite believe what you're hearing, then don't believe it, but do ask for more proof! People are often a little worried about that one – why is that? Perhaps we think we will upset our guides (more on them later) if we ask for proof time and time again, or perhaps we think we'll get such proof that we will never recover or even that an angel will be sent to whisk us away to someplace where we can't cause any bother. But can you really see a spiritual guide, a spiritually advanced soul, throwing a hissy fit because you asked whether or not they were real, then popping off to the spiritual guides' common room to compare notes with the rest and giggle at just how silly you were?

Ask, ask again, and if you're still not convinced, ask even more.

When my guide moved in, I wasn't convinced. He was a Native American and I wasn't sure that's what I wanted. Get me! Not what I wanted! It makes me chuckle now to think of the ego involved in that little scenario, me with my face on, recognizing a new guide had in fact made himself known but because he was a stereotype refusing to have any of it and even trying to clothe him in other garments when I saw him in meditation, just a like a psychic Action Man doll, attempting to make him fit what I wanted, not what he in fact was.

Finally I asked for proof. Here's a list of some of the things it took for me to stop asking:

○   Three mediums told me, 'You have a lovely big Indian with you, feathers and all!'

○   I was given a CD of Native American music by a friend who would be hard pushed to give away her breath, never mind something like a CD, but she gave it with a smile on her face.

○   I was given a statue of a Native American out of the blue by a client.

○   Turquoise jewellery was given to me by two fans – that's turquoise Native American jewellery, if you hadn't already guessed.

Apart from sticking me in a tepee and dressing me in bearskins, there was little more that could be done to prove that I indeed had a Native American guide, and in the end I accepted it and I love him.

The secret is to ask for proof, then accept it when it comes your way.

'It Doesn't Balance'

When I was working in a little hotel in Portsmouth I sometimes, in fact very often, found myself late duty manager, on the rota as LDM. There it was, six days this week, five the next: 'David, LDM'! This meant I was, as you have probably figured out by now, working late as the manager on duty, which of course also meant I locked up after the last guest had left the bar. Late.

As midnight approached, I was regularly up to date on any work I had outstanding and had walked around the premises so many times my feet were aching and still room 14 was swinging off that last brandy – and it's apparently rude to set up breakfast when guests are still on their after-dinner brandy...

This was in the dark ages when computers were still relatively new and I didn't have one of my own so had to share, and this was an ideal time to do it as nobody else wanted to draw a house or spend hours playing solitaire in the middle of the night.

My Qabalah group had been working on a technique called channelling where you simply sit down and link into your spiritual guide, spiritual self or ascended master (if you're at that point) and let go, writing down your conversation with said being or saying it out loud. I got the concept but hadn't thought of it as being much use, as it was the same stuff that constantly came out: love each other, you can be who you want to be, we are here for you, don't eat yellow snow...

So one night I was on the computer, gazing into space, as you do, and I typed on the screen: *'What is the point?'*

Then from nowhere I typed back: 'What would you like the point to be?'

It had just come to me, that answer was just in my head, so I carried on: *'I would like to know why I am here.'*

'What do you want to be here for?'

At this point I was thinking, 'Here we go again, gobbledegook without any rhyme or reason,' so I got specific:

'Who are you?'

'Shouldn't the question be "Who are *you*?"'

'Who are you?'

'We are the White Brotherhood. Who are you?

'I am David.'

'Is that all that you are? David?'

'It's all that I know.'

'We know that isn't true, we know you understand you are more than David. You are the sum of all you have been and what you can be. This we know you know.'

'Why do you always seem to talk funny?!'

'We don't talk funny, you listen funny.'

'Ha, ha.'

(Now I really was losing it – I was sharing jokes with my computer, which had been taken over by some otherworld comedian! Great!)

'David, you are on a path that will take you to places far and wide but no matter where you go you must know that you are always connected to us and can call on us whenever you need.'

'How?'

'You already know how: think and it becomes.'

'Every thought becomes a thing?'

'Indeed it does.'

'How do I know you are real?'

'You don't.'

'That's a rubbish answer.'

'By the end of this year you will have moved, you will be better placed to do what you set out to do when you first incarnated and we will stand behind you when you need to speak and be heard. OK?'

'So what now?'

There was silence and I felt the connection was gone. Then in trotted the barman with the night's takings and those immortal words: 'It doesn't balance.' Tell me about it.

That night I lay in bed wondering what that had all been about. It was the first of many channelling experiences I had at this time and each one seemed to be on a different topic. Some were very universal and others were a lot more personal, but as time went on I forgot about the computer and accepted the White Brotherhood was there whether I wrote down what I was hearing or not.

When I teach I often have a schedule with me, a security blanket. I usually stray from that original plan, though, and more often than not I don't use it at all, I just pay attention and listen to what comes next. The secret is to use your techniques and open those channels, but don't forget to go with the flow of the universe, the flow of energy if you like.

So how can you understand energy more?

Chapter 4

Energy Warrior

You never know how or when you're going to be asked for help. There is of course e-mail and sometimes there's the friend of a friend who asks for assistance in some way or other, and then there's notes through the door! Not a usual one for me, but there was good reason for one a while back.

Some time ago I had my kitchen redone – the usual chaos to make way for a shiny work surface or three – and as a result there was some debris to be taken care of. I called in a local company to get rid of all the old units and bricks, and a few months later the owner of the company, Mark, put a note through my letterbox to ask me to call him concerning a problem his mother was experiencing in a property she had recently moved into. How could I refuse? (I know that's a bad joke, but it's all I have.)

A date was set and off I went.

On a Mission

As I put the address into the satellite navigation system, the name stuck in my mind: the street had the word 'mission' in it. Immediately my subconscious threw up the now familiar pictures and this time it was of monks and a graveyard. I knew I was about to deal with a collective energy. Perhaps there would be the odd one or two individuals who would stand out, but in my heart I recognized years of energy built up as time went by.

I pulled up at the house. It was a very pleasant home with two bedrooms, a lovely lounge and a gorgeous garden at the back, but it felt as though I was walking through toffee to get to it. The energy was not particularly threatening, just dense.

I went on and was greeted by Mark and other members of his family and of course his lovely, lovely mum. Unbeknown to me, Mark's father had died that very week and my heart went out to her. Having recently lost my own father, I found she reminded me of my own mum. I asked if it would be better if I called another time, but they asked me to stay and she told me her experiences.

She described seeing a woman in her bedroom, the curtains in the room moving to an almost horizontal position and her bathrobe, which was hanging behind the door, moving of its own accord. Some family members had stayed there that week and had experienced some odd things themselves.

Now I hear this sort of thing a lot and as much I believe in the astral worlds and the reluctance of spirits to move on, I am not one for believing everything people tell me. I do need to see or hear for myself how the energy is behaving before I make a judgement. Mark's mum was, however, very bright, very rational and had been dealing with this before her husband had passed, so it wasn't likely to have been caused by grief. I had to see for myself.

The main energy source seemed to be the bedroom, so clearly that's where I had to go. I went on my own to sit in the room and to open up my own energy to see or feel what I would see or feel. I opened my chakras (more on this later), protected the space and myself and waited.

At first there was nothing other than that sticky energy. I call it 'wearing my toffee hat' – it's as though my brain won't connect the way it usually does. Then I became more aware and through that thickness in my head I began to see the forms of a woman and a young girl in the room and a man who was lurking by the door. They didn't appear to notice me and that was just fine, I wasn't about to announce my arrival just yet. I opened up my clairaudience and listened to the house; it was noisy but there was an air of melancholy about it.

It was time to uncloak myself and make a stand. I turned up the light, said my Qabalistic prayer of protection out loud and waited.

The woman was the first to turn in my direction and come towards me. The child hid beneath one of the beds and the man stood his ground by the door. Over the years I have seen it all with spirits – they have changed shape or looked threatening, all sorts – but I am fully aware I have more to fear from the living than the dead and so with 100 per cent faith in my protection I stood up to the woman and suggested she might want to leave.

She wasn't convinced.

I asked them all to go, to no avail. They seemed intent upon staying, which wasn't a problem in itself, it was the fact that they were interfering in the life of this lovely lady that was a bit of a bother, so I began a ritual to help them see the light.

I firmly believe we do not have the power to force spirits out, as they too have their own views and wishes, but we can thicken the veil between this world and the next so that we can't see them or they us, and we can also reason with them and help them make the right decision. Many people wave their hands about and affirm, 'This place is clear,' in about two seconds flat, but they do it with no real knowledge or understanding and without even a phone call to check how things are going a few days later.

So I had a battle on my hands, or rather on my chakras! The energy was draining, so I went out into the garden for a new perspective. That only seemed to make it worse. The ground beneath my feet felt alive and I wondered if there was something more to this than the obvious. Earth energies seemed to be feeding the house, making it come alive as it were, and the name kept going around in my head: 'Mission, mission, mission.'

I asked about the name and it appeared to come from a small tin church that had once stood there, nothing fancy but a place of worship and of emotion, emotion that might still be built into the ground. I also felt hands reaching up from the earth, a sign for me that there were unmarked graves in the area – as yet unconfirmed, but how do you confirm it without digging the whole place up?

Part of this work is to know when to call in specialized help, not to assume you know it all, which I never do, and I am not afraid to either admit it or ask for help.

So I called Tony Ainsworth.

Earth Energy

Tony is a very talented healer dealing with Earth energies and I have known him clear negativity around me in seconds as well as help me realize that I need to put a lot more effort into keeping my own space clean and clear. There's a full explanation of his beliefs from the man himself at the back of the book, but essentially, as he says:

There is a very simplistic approach available to take with Earth energy, and that's if it's not balanced it's wrong, and the ultimate ambition of any Earth energy practitioner is to achieve perfect balance of Earth energy in buildings, spaces or areas and ultimately in people.

Tony doesn't have to be anywhere near a property to tune in or to help, so I called him up and we began trying to shift the energies over the telephone.

Tony asked me if there was any stagnant water near the property. There was a fishpond that needed some attention. He asked me to stand near it and to offer up some energy towards the water, which I did. I am Reiki trained and find that discipline a lovely healing practice, but I am of the mind that energy is energy no matter how you dress it up.

When I was happy the energy was lighter, I told Tony so. He then asked me to walk around the garden and concentrate on sending healing energy to the Earth and he would do the same.

As I began, the oddest thing happened: I burped and burped and burped some more! Tony told me that often happens as energy is released and hand on heart I can honestly say I have never experienced anything like it before!

So I burped my way round the garden and started to feel things get lighter. Tony asked me if I had sensed a child, to which I replied that I had, and he then told me she was a little scared by it all, so I should try to reassure her. I focused in on her and offered white reassuring light and she seemed to relax.

I knew what Tony was doing was removing the energy the spirits were feeding on, removing their need to be there if you like, and as I watched I could see grey energy turning to white. The very large wooden door into the garden was ajar and there was no wind. I said, 'I think they are leaving in their droves,' and as I said that the door slammed – something it did again later when I was talking to Mark and his family in the kitchen. Was it just a freak breeze or the final act of an energy that wasn't too happy to be asked to leave?

Tony said he would continue to work on the property and I assured him I would do the same. I went into the bedroom, which now seemed lighter, and invoked the four great archangels for protection, Raphael for Air, Michael for Fire, Gabriel for Water and Uriel for Earth, seeing them standing around the property with their backs towards it, facing out in a defensive position.

I asked Mark's mum to go into the room and see if she felt any change. She said it felt lighter and so did everyone else who went in. Job done, off I went, happy to help, but it doesn't end there...

Some weeks later Mark informed me that his mum was still having difficulties with the woman in particular and as I was away travelling I asked Tony for his advice. He suggested the house be emptied of all people, the electricity switched off for at least an hour and nobody return until after that length of time at the very least.

Mark duly did this, something I never thought of, but it makes perfect sense – energy from batteries often goes when on paranormal investigations so there must be a correlation between electrical energy and paranormal activity – and when he re-entered the property, it felt much calmer. However, it is an ongoing process. As Tony would say, no one person has a divine right to move spirit on, it's an energetic process.

Change your Life

To see energy at work on a more personal level in your own life, think for a moment about your own spiritual journey. Along the way your friendships will change, if they haven't already, and you yourself will change, you will appear to be lighter – and by that I don't mean you will drop ten pounds, although you very well might, what I mean is all those things that once bothered you no longer will, all those people who would once have had you gritting your teeth will no longer get to you in the same way. In fact they may not even be around to try.

Life cannot change without change – it's an obvious one really, but how many of us stop and actively encourage change into our life? When was the last time you felt things couldn't go on and were prepared not only to think about things, to wonder and dream, to create them in your head, but to actively go out and get on with making them happen, whatever the obstacles?

Your mind is a powerful thing. Your subconscious mind can prevent you from moving on, but harnessed correctly it can be the greatest friend you will ever have, as it will bring you new challenges that will help you grow. And all it takes is to constantly feed it what you want and avoid feeding it what you don't.

Try this very simple exercise and see just what I mean.

Get a large piece of card, about A3 at least.

Now look through some magazines and photographs and stick all those things you want onto it; make this your 'future board'. (Not your wish board – wishing leaves it wishy-washy.)

Put images on your board of all the things you want to have in your future, and as you do so, let your imagination, your subconscious, take you into that world where they all exist. Enjoy the view, know it's all there waiting for you.

Now put your board somewhere where you will see it every day, even if it's just for a few moments. That's all it takes for your subconscious to get the message and for the universe to start providing you with opportunities to make it happen.

The secret? Change begets change. So see what you want and create those opportunities.

Chapter 5

A Little More Guidance

We can do a lot for ourselves, but of course we do all need a little help from time to time as well. There are many ways and many teachers out there, and not all are as earthly or indeed as earthy as Tony Ainsworth! Some are around us all of the time and even though we can't always see them they are trying to ease our path. In fact, one of the most common questions I am asked is: 'How do I contact my spirit guide?'

Spiritual Navigation Systems

The reason so many people would like to contact their spirit guide is that they're feeling a little lost, wondering which direction to go in. Wouldn't it be great if all you had to do was put in your direction and set your spiritual guidance system to 'Go'? But many of us find ourselves wondering what to do for the best, for ourselves and others – what if, maybe, woulda, coulda, shoulda...

Your spiritual guide is your navigation system, someone who holds the map, and if you can get a little closer to listening to their guidance, you'll be well on your way to that new direction you seek – your destiny perhaps?

But first things first.

I constantly say, 'Begin at the beginning.' By that I mean, 'Don't see the massive task you think is ahead of you, start by seeing the first step, because, after all, without taking it you're really never going to get anywhere!' So the first step is to identify why you want to meet your spiritual guide, or in fact guides. Let me explain.

Just as in life you have lots of friends, so you have different guides, some of them more knowledgeable than others, and, just as in life, you go to different ones for different things – you wouldn't go to your best mate for advice on something technical at work, would you, and of course you wouldn't go to your boss to ask what he thought about that bloke over there who keeps giving you the come hither!

Knowing which guides you may encounter will help you identify whom you are working with and what they are trying to communicate, and then, when you need to ask for help, you will know where to go.

Earthly Guides

It often surprises people when I say that the first level of guides is usually right in front of you: they are your family and friends. These are, after all, spiritual beings just like you, spiritual beings having a human experience and more than capable of advising you on important matters from their soul rather than their personality, given half a chance – so don't forget to ask! Remember your spiritual guides are always going to be around you, too, which means your friends will also be around *them*, so you get double bubble if you stop and listen!

Lifetime Guide

Next on the list is your lifetime guide. They were with you at the moment you were born and will be with you when you shake off this mortal coil. They are usually someone with a past-life interest who knows you very well indeed. They know the true you, the inner workings of your soul, why you have incarnated and the lessons you want to get from that journey. They sometimes present themselves to you in fancy dress – that's usually a clue to which life you know them from or what sort of energy you are working with. For example, my lifetime guide is a Native American. I was his wife in another life, and boy, does it show! He rarely speaks, but he nods a lot and he's very good at giving disapproving looks!

These lifetime guides have an overall picture and, like all guides, they can't directly influence you, but they can put suggestions and ideas to you. It's whether or not you want to take them or even see them that's the challenge. Don't worry, they aren't sticking to you every second of every day, but they know when you need them and they check back with you all the time.

Doorkeeper

Next is your doorkeeper. Doorkeepers are protectors, they stand in front of you to keep your crown chakra safe. By that I simply mean they won't let any negative energy affect you as long as you keep yourself under some sort of control. They don't work very well if you are under the influence of drugs or alcohol, which isn't any judgement on those who use them to excess, it's just telling it how I see it.

These massive beings are often scary in appearance. They present as warriors and can be either male or female. My own doorkeeper shows himself as an executioner and I wouldn't want to meet him on a dark night, I can tell you! When I work, particularly in haunted locations, I see him standing in front of me to strengthen my protection and I sometimes feel him step in when I am confronted by a particularly angry energy.

Personality Guides

Your mates and your family are sort of personality guides, but on the astral planes this role sometimes falls to a relation who has crossed, someone who wants to make sure that you're fine on an earthly level. They are comforters and provide those little signs that reassure us – Granny's perfume in the air, a reassuring feeling when you see a photograph of them or something that just makes you smile when you need it most.

This is one way to recognize your personality guide: they have something about them that identifies their role. My personality guide shows up wearing a suit, a blue suit, and on occasion he rides a motorbike! How personality is that?

These guides are there to make sure you get on with those earthly tasks like eating and putting a roof over your head, and occasionally they will bring some interesting people your way to help move you on if you get a little stuck.

Teacher Guides

When you begin to think a little more about your spiritual journey and a little less about how you're going to afford that handbag, a little light comes on and it begins to attract teacher guides. Teacher guides move in and out – they may stay with you for a month or perhaps years – but their influence is very strong and they have definite ideas about getting you to see your potential.

The first one I was ever aware of was with me for about 32 years. It took her that long to get me to the door of my spiritual training – more my fault than hers, I suspect! The experience I had with her was one of the most profound of my spiritual journey to date. I had been told a guide was leaving me and I sort of knew it was a woman, but nothing prepared me for the vision I was to see. I awoke at about three in the morning and at the end of my bed was a European woman wearing a bright blue sari, and it wasn't just bright blue, it was *bright blue*, the like of which I had never seen before. She smiled, blew me a kiss and left. I cried myself to sleep because she'd gone and when I woke up the next morning I felt blessed by the experience but bereft, as if someone had died. Remembering that event can still bring tears to my eyes after all these years. I suspect she, too, was someone I once knew well.

These teacher guides are there to help open up a true calling within and they are what I call the 'right here, right now guides', that's to say they are teachers for right here, right now and will stay with you until you have learned all that you can from them.

Soul Guides

Next up the ladder are soul guides. Imagine your whole being is a bumper car, a dodgem – go with me on this! The grid that provides the energy is the cosmos and the bit that attaches itself to it is your spirit, so your spirit is always connected. Now think about the dodgem car itself as your soul, a vehicle that gets its energy from that link and that link is always there. Now imagine your personality is the driver. You see where I am going with this? You're here, there and everywhere, when actually all you have to do is let go and let the soul and spirit do the driving for you. Not easy – that's the whole point, I guess – but easier when you make contact with those soul guides.

These guides also present in costume to let you know what sort of energy they bring. They may not have a past-life link. They look after many souls and usually move in when you're on a path to higher spiritual awareness but not exclusively. We always have them, though, it's our awareness that changes when we get closer to them, which leads me to answer that question: 'How do I contact my spirit guide?' If it's your soul guide you're after, and it usually is, you do it by raising your vibration through the work that you do and one day there they are!

Masters

I had a real problem with the whole hierarchy of guides and master this, that and the other, and when my teacher spoke to us of masters, I was at my limit. It seemed that the spiritual worlds were run like a major company, with supervisors, managers, managing directors and of course the big company director at the top of it all. And the corporate world was something I saw as earthly and surely not worthy of my spiritual journey!

But then I thought about it. Without structure, there would be chaos; without defined roles, how would we know whom to turn to and why? And maybe, just maybe, the reason we have such structures here on Earth is another confirmation of 'as above, so below'. Then I thought about how it all worked and realized that the most successful companies had good communication up and down the chain of command, a chain that let the lowliest worker have a say, and I settled into the idea.

So, masters. I was called a spiritual master on television in Australia once and I spat my dummy out at the interviewer. If you're going to use the word, attach it to beings at the level of Jesus of Nazareth, Buddha, Krishna, etc. They are true masters, and there are many more you won't have heard of, but that's for another time. In the here and now, recognize that if a master moves in to help with your teaching, you truly have put the effort in!

Communicating with your Guides

So how do you ask your guides for help?

Well, you ask your guides for help – it's not rocket science!

In fact, the secret to becoming more aware of your guides is communication. Even if you feel a bit silly asking for help from someone you can't see or hear, it's the start of getting the support you want.

By asking for help, you give permission for your guides to put ideas and thoughts into your head or to put people in front of you that will show you the way. But this comes with a warning: if you ask for help and then constantly ignore it, they will withdraw until it seems you're more likely to listen. It's my belief that we are told three times, then they step back, so it's up to you whether you take action and go with what you feel, no matter where the prompting comes from, or not. Yes, that's 'feel'. If you're expecting your guides to pop up through the floor and say, 'This way, please,' you are likely to be sorely disappointed. Some people claim to see their guides physically every day. That hasn't been my experience, so if you do, then well done, you. For most of us they communicate through a feeling, a sensation that they are around. For me, that suggests that I stop and wait for any impressions that come to me. I do of course meditate specifically to meet my guides and to ask questions of them as well.

RIGHT GUIDE FOR THE RIGHT JOB
To recap then, before I show you a very simple way to communicate with your guides:

○ *Earthly:* Friends and family, used for advice on earthly matters.

○ *Lifetime:* A supportive guide with a link to the past and to the plan!

○ *Doorkeeper:* A protector always there defending your energy.

○ *Personality:* On hand for advice about your love life, mortgage and earthly dramas.

○ *Teacher:* For when you're learning new skills and remembering old skills. They move in and out.

○ *Soul:* For life's bigger questions. When you're ready, they'll be there.

○ *Masters:* Highly evolved, these guides are waiting for you to pursue a spiritual path.

So much help is available and you're never alone, and if you know what level your question is aimed at (and you do already), you will know which guide to ask for help.

Asking

How do you ask? You can simply ask, either out loud or in your head, and know that you have been heard. If, however, you want to take the time to build stronger relationships with your guides, then I would suggest you take some time out to meditate and lift yourself up to their level.

Here's a very simple visualization that could help you:

Remember to switch off phones and remove any distractions.

Relax, relax and close your eyes.

Take a deep breath in and as you release it, let your body relax even more.

✪ ✪ ✪ ✪

Now imagine you're in a forest. Build it around you and let it truly be there. Touch the plants, smell the air and hear the noise of the forest around you.

Ahead of you, you will see a path. Take it, it's a familiar and safe path for you to follow.

An animal may dart out or fly around you. This is your animal guide, a guide that represents a facet of you. What is it? What does it mean?

Walk along the path until you come to a clearing, well-tended lawn with flowers planted around its border, with everything in the brightest colours you can imagine.

You may see a giant oak tree at one end. This time it's not where you're heading, this time you're heading towards the right of the tree, towards a small plain white picket fence with a gate in it. Go through the gate.

Now you find yourself in a garden, a rose garden, and dotted around you are statues of Roman and Greek gods and goddesses, symbols of the different facets of humanity and representing the planets that surround us.

The beauty of this place is almost overwhelming, but carry on. Walk along a heavenly scented path through the garden.

Eventually you come across a garden bench, simple in its design and perfectly placed by a wishing well. Take a seat.

The bell above the wishing well rings once, only once, and you know it's a sign for your guide to visit.

Look up and see them approach you and let them sit beside you, ready to commune.

Ask your questions, and in asking and receiving you will know which guide this is.

Take your time. If they offer you a gift, accept it. See what it is and where they place it. Remember all these images are important and when you think about it later you will get even more information from your meeting with your guide.

When you're ready, prepare to leave.

Thank your guide and even though parting is difficult you know you have to return to your earthly challenges and seek those blessings your guide has pointed out to you.

Walk back along your path and out of the gate, closing it behind you.

Your animal guide may be there to show you through the clearing and back into the forest where your journey began. Follow them.

As you walk through the forest, say farewell and thank you to your animal and then carry on through the forest.

Now let it fade away and bring your consciousness back into the here and now.

Wiggle your fingers and toes, get ready to write down your experience and remember to put the kettle on and have a biscuit!

Your guides are magical and wonderful beings, but there are three things you mustn't lose sight of: every one of them was once where you are now, every one of them has gone through all those human experiences you may be having difficulties with and every one of them is happy to help you.

For *Real People, Real Past Lives* I did many regressions and in one of them a young lady saw herself in a past life as a guide. It's not uncommon. So I will share with you yet another secret: there is every chance that you have been a guide and every chance you will be again. A past life as a guide? Why not? You could have been a soldier, a sailor or a cabinet maker, so why not a spirit guide? What I do know is past lives hold more answers than the obvious.

Tick,
Tock

On the subject of past, present and future, time is relative, but is it also linear or is it circular or is it both at the same time? Who knows, but what I do know is that here on Earth we have watches and clocks and when it's eight thirty and the show started at eight, you're late.

When you are dealing with your guides and teachers, timing is everything. If you're having a group meditation at seven and someone blusters in at seven ten, it's clearly going to affect things and you just wouldn't do it. Why then would it be acceptable to send the universe a signal that you're going to meditate at seven and you would like your guides to help you on your quest, and then turn up at eight?

You could say time is relative and surely guides would know you were going to be there at eight anyway, but does that send the right message to *you*? Do you then begin to think that sloppy practice is OK because your guides will know and sort it out, so you needn't bother? But you should bother because your psychic behaviour has a knock-on effect on your physical life. If you're late to your group, late with your written work and late with your meditations, you will be playing catch up forever.

It's a mistake to assume that your spiritual and psychic life is detached from your physical one; it is not. Good practice results in a tidy life – secret.

Chapter 6

Lorna: Past, Present, Future

One of the things I often hear when I do past-life workshops or seminars is that people have enough problems with this life without worrying about the past. It makes me smile, smile, smile like a smiley thing. When I ask where they think some of their problems come from, the stock answer is usually: 'I don't know, they're just there.' So these problems just manifest out of thin air, do they? They come out of nowhere to have a huge impact in our life? Or they just happen along the way as people interact with other people?

I wouldn't disagree with that last statement, actually, but what if what you're actually seeing is souls interacting with souls rather than personalities interacting with other personalities? What if those you can't live with, or can't live without, hold more than just this-life issues? What if they were with you in a former life and you're working out some differences as well as enjoying being together now? In order to learn what you're here to learn, wouldn't you choose to have help from those who had travelled with you for many incarnations? And in turn wouldn't you want to be near them to help with their path, no matter how tough that might be – that's *no matter how tough that might be*?

'Karma' is the word of the moment when it comes to past-life work: the law of cause and effect, the idea that what you do gets returned to you. Actually, it's probably more about balance, about an action having an opposite or equal reaction that shows us how we make others feel by getting us to feel it ourselves. Have you got that? I tickle you, you tickle me back and we're even. You pinch me, I pinch you harder and I have something coming to me! This doesn't mean to say you have to tiptoe round life attempting to be a good soul so that you don't create anything you may have to pay for later – you can be a good soul and still make mistakes. I make plenty and I like to think that no matter how grumpy I get, I am a good soul!

For me, the secret to karma is action. If you procrastinate, you won't negate any karma, and although some say you won't create any either, I would disagree with that. By doing nothing you create karma through your refusal to get involved, so why not have a go?

Past-life theories are many and varied. There's more on them in my books *Past, Present and Future* and *Real People, Real Past Lives* if you want to investigate them in more detail, but in this book I want to show that esoteric principles aren't detached from your life, they are part of it, and they can offer a solution to your problems if you look for it or ask for it.

Lorna, Chris and Lee

When a book is published it makes good sense to move around the country promoting your work with book signings, something I really enjoy, as I get the opportunity to meet those who read the books and not only hear what they think of the last one but also what questions they have that I can address in future projects, be they publishing or teaching. Everyone, remember, has a message for us and it's down to us to listen, and so it was one wet day in Newbury in November 2008, when I met Lorna and Chris. They had come along to have their book signed and asked if they could talk to me afterwards.

When they did, Lorna told me her young son Lee had been killed in a car crash. Unusually, she didn't ask me if he was OK and if I could communicate with him to let him know his family was thinking of him. What she did ask was: 'Will I have more time with him in my next incarnation?'

Those words bounced around my head for a few seconds and from nowhere my mouth opened and I suggested a past-life regression for her and her husband. I really had no idea how it could help, but I trusted my gut instinct.

Lorna graciously accepted and a date was made for some weeks later.

Joint Regression

Lorna and Chris welcomed me to their beautiful home and made me feel at ease. They clearly had a very strong relationship and I was moved by the love they showed each other and delighted to be able to help, even if, to be honest, I didn't have a clue how it was going to go. Just trusting in the process, I asked them both if they would like a separate regression or a joint one. Doing a regression for two people at once offers the opportunity to see if there is a shared former life that is having an impact on this one. It's a spiritual 'buy one, get one free'.

Lorna and Chris opted for the joint regression. I asked them to make themselves comfortable and to hold hands, relax and follow my voice, and used creative visualization to help them access their former lives. I will describe this technique for you at the end of this chapter. For now, let's stick with Lorna and Chris.

David: When you're ready, Chris, can you tell me what you're wearing on your feet?

Chris: Sackcloth, nothing more than cloth.

D: What about you, Lorna?

Lorna: Sandals. I have sandals on my feet, just plain leather sandals.

D: What else are you wearing, Lorna?

L: A dress that's like sackcloth, nothing fancy.

D: What can you see, Chris?

C: I can see a woman.

D: Look into her eyes for me, look straight into her eyes. Do you recognize her?

C: No.

D: What are you doing, Lorna?

L: I am walking by a river. I am about 23 and my name begins with 'M'. I think I'm in Yugoslavia.

D: What are you doing by the river?

L: Catching fish, or trying to!

D: What are you doing, Chris?

C: I am outdoors walking by some trees, heading towards some woods. I am about 30 years old and in France. I feel it is the seventeenth century.

(It was now obvious they were not in the same life but I had a feeling they were part of each other's regression. Perhaps the two lives being seen each held a key to events in this one.)

D: Lorna, is there anyone with you?

L: I have two children with me. I have black hair. The father of my children isn't with me. I don't know where he is.

D: What are you doing, Chris?

C: I am finding something to make toys or tools with – I'm not sure. I am looking for wood.

D: What's happening now, Lorna?

L: I am walking into a town, down a street and into a house. There's a stove there with a fireplace and a table in the middle of the room. It's 1860 and there are just the two children and me in the house, nobody else.

D: Do you recognize either of the children? Look into their eyes – they never change, the essence never changes.

L: I don't recognize them.

(For the sceptics among us, if Lorna had been making it up, wouldn't she have seen her son in one of her children's eyes? Wasn't that what she wanted? Why wasn't he there?)

D: What's happening with you, Chris?

C: I am in the woods, digging for something, but whatever it is, I can't find it.

D: Can you move on a little, Chris, and tell me where you find yourself?

C: I am in a shed. I live in this shed. I don't seem to have any family at all.

D: What's happening with you, Lorna?

L: A man has walked through the door. He's my husband. He puts a bag down. It has logs in it, logs for the fire.

C: I make enough to live on, just about, but can't see any family.

L: I am taking the kids out of the door. I think I am taking them to school – no, wait, I am taking them away on a boat.

D: Watch what happens, Lorna, whilst I find out more about Chris.

C: Lots of people are selling things at the market, lots of people are in an open market area with tables, all selling things. I'm doing the same and I do all right. I am going back to the woods.

D: What's happening now, Lorna?

L: I seem to be somewhere hot. It seems like Africa. It was too much for me in Yugoslavia, I couldn't stand it, there was nothing there for me. I have come here without my husband. I sell fruit to make a living.

D: What's happening with you, Chris?

C: It's night-time, I'm with some people from the market and we are drinking and eating, having a good time. I can see a fire – it's my shed, it's burning, my shed is burning!

D: What's happening now, Chris?

C: I'm running towards it and trying to put it out. But I can't put it out, it's overwhelming me and I'm collapsing. There seems to be someone feeding the fire, making it worse. I am pushed into it and die.

D: OK, Chris, you don't have to feel it, just see yourself surrounded by light and sit there in that light. Feel calm and at peace and take in all the energy around you.

D: Now Lorna, where are you?

L: It's two years on and I can see a cliff in the distance.

D: What's happening now?

L: I'm jumping off the cliff. My children have already died and I have nothing to live for. They died in a fire. They loved me and I loved them... We will always be together.

D: Go into the light, Lorna. Go into it and surround yourself with it.

D: Now both of you sit there and wait for any guides to come to you, any astrals or people from that life to make themselves known to you. I will withdraw and leave you to it. Let me know when you have finished.

Evaluation

At this point I was wondering what it was all about. Lorna and Chris had experienced separate lives and neither had seemed to go to a time or a place that was in any way relevant to the situation that had brought them to this moment. But I have learned through the years that the spiritual worlds move in their own way and their own time and I knew I had to trust in the process.

As I waited for Lorna and Chris to finish evaluating their lives, I opened my own inner vision to see where Lee was. He was standing beside his mother, holding her hand, and as I watched, Lorna opened her hand as if to welcome him. He looked at me and smiled, a smile full of wisdom and strength, a smile that said, 'Thank you,' and showed that he was at peace and on his own journey. Wiping away my tears, I asked Lorna and Chris if they were ready to leave their past lives and brought their awareness back into the room.

They were both energetically worn out and Lorna in particular looked shattered, but she had a smile on her face. She said she realized now that Lee would never be far away from her and even though he wasn't in her life physically she could still love him and feel his love around her.

Both Chris and Lorna had had moments of clarity that I hope last forever and it was my absolute pleasure, in fact privilege, to be part of it. I thanked them both and asked them to think about things and get back to me when they were ready.

Later Lorna e-mailed me. Things had really changed for her:

I still feel great, in fact I feel happy. I still wake up every day with no pain to my heart. Instead I feel so blessed Lee was and still is my son...

I still find it hard to understand the change in myself since the regression – it's unbelievable how someone can lose such a precious beautiful son like Lee and cope so well after just one sitting. How can so much devastation and depression turn into hope and contentment?

I never would have imagined I could feel this strong and in control just two years after the loss...

I have dreamed of Lee a few times since the regression. I think it's because I am more at peace now. I think he comes closer to me now because he knows I am stronger.

Gratitude

Though the past-life regression I had been hoping to help Lorna see she had shared many lives with Lee and there were likely to be many more to come, but that's not what I got. Instead I got a complete change in Lorna because she saw how much Lee loved her and she was grateful for that. In life we can be grateful for so many things and what they are depends on our personal circumstances, but the important thing is to be grateful every day.

I am grateful for Lorna, Chris and of course Lee – grateful that Lorna and Chris showed me just how magical our spiritual selves can be when needs must, grateful for the lessons they gave me and the faith it gave me to carry on at a time when I was wondering whether or not it was worth all the hassle you sometimes get. Lorna's e-mail was worth a million times more than anything I can think of.

Living with Loss

By her next e-mail, Lorna was starting a healing course with a Reiki master, had joined a development circle, had booked onto an angel workshop and was also hoping to do healing with crystals. She certainly seemed to be throwing herself into a great many things, though I felt sure that in time she would settle down to what really resonated with her. In the meantime, what I loved about her e-mails was the enthusiasm and the brightness in her writing. She also highlighted some very good points that are useful to anyone's development: try before you buy, find good teachers, get involved with a group, as you will learn from the people around you, and above all, have enthusiasm!

Some weeks later she wrote again, explaining what she had learned:

I now have learned to live a spiritual life with Lee and a physical life with Chris, Deena and James [her other children].

Living without Lee was something I could not and would not cope with. How can you live without the children you love and adore?

I have now realized I don't have to live without him but I live with him in a totally different way... I hope when other mothers read my story they can also realize ... that when the physical person is not there, the person is still there in spirit.

I live alongside my beautiful son now and I will do for the rest of my life.

Lorna makes a wonderfully simple point in her e-mail: we live among those we have loved and lost. We all do this. They never leave our memories and sometimes we feel them around us, but the point is, do we pay attention? When a thought comes to you or that wee still voice reminds you of a loved one's sayings or phrases, when a perfume wafts your way or a piece of music awakens a memory, they are with you. Many times I am asked what the secret is to hearing them pass by. It's simply to listen.

Remember, energy is everywhere and is in everything, so you are your loved ones and they are you and you'll know when they are around. You don't have to be from a long line of mediums, you don't have to be the seventh son of a seventh son, you don't have to wear orange and own more crystals than anyone else, you just have to be part of it all – and you already are.

Past and Present

It was some months later when Lorna got back in touch and she told me more about her regression and the links with her current life:

I knew Lee would die from the moment I knew I was expecting him. I dreamed he would die young, so for 21 years I lived in fear.

My regression showed that in the past I had two children who died, and in this life I lost Lee and Emma [Lee's girlfriend, who died with him in the crash]. *Again, two children died.*

I have feared cliffs and heights all my life and never knew why. Now I do.

I must admit I thought my regression was a tad boring at first until I really thought about it.

In this life I have always been completely dedicated to my family and that is all that's been important to me. I work alone and I have wonderful friends, but I would be happy if I had no friends, as my family has always been enough for me – strange, I know, but I felt this also in the regression.

I knew that the man who came in with the wood for the fire was Chris, although I could not see his face.

(I didn't say at the time, as he was in the seventeenth century in his regression, but I felt it was his build.)

Killing myself in my past life took me away from the devastation of the deaths of my children. In this life, that's how I felt too – that I could not live with the pain. But since the regression, that pain has gone. I can now see where to go and what I have to do.

I spend no time thinking of the man who killed Lee and Emma. I realize he is on his own journey.

Lee and Emma walk by my side and I will carry that knowledge and strength with me until the day I die (something I now have no fear of).

How something as simple as a regression can be so powerful is amazing.

The most wonderful statement of this e-mail was Lorna's forgiveness of the man who caused the accident that took her son from her. It's a truly empowering thing to be able to forgive and it's not easy for many of us. Who knows how you or I would react given the circumstances Lorna had to endure? It's a great testament to her spirit and her spiritual growth that she has passed into this phase.

Incidentally, Lee's surname was Makepeace. Make Peace.

Lorna's e-mail also highlighted something that's common to a lot of regressions – you don't get it until you get it! Sometimes information takes time to filter through and to make sense, and expecting it all to make sense in a couple of hours shouldn't be up there on your list. From personal experience I can tell you that sometimes it can take months, if not years, for the light to go on!

Past Lives and You

So how about you? Is there someone in your life you think you have shared a past life with? I know it's a subject I have covered before, so this time I want to give you a technique that takes things to another level, something that's easy to do but may start you thinking about your relationships with those around you, everyone from family to friends and all points in between.

Lorna's case was very dramatic and an extreme example of how past-life links can help you in the here and now. For most of us they aren't as severe, but thanks to Lorna's courage and willingness to share her experience I hope the possibilities are clearer to you. If you're having relationships issues or problems with family, you may find an answer in a past life.

Ordinarily, past-life therapy is a case of having a regression and seeing what occurs, but if you need to know something in order to understand what's happening now, you need to ask for a life that's particularly relevant to those issues, a life that shows you where that dynamic has come from. The best advice is always to seek a therapist that's recommended and take someone with you – a good friend or even the person you want to know more about. Be careful with that, though – make sure they are open to it and know it will bring up points for discussion that may not always be comfortable.

If you can't find a therapist you feel comfortable with or you want to try to find out on your own, I have a visualization that may help. There's that word again: visualization! Don't worry, you know it simply means seeing pictures and letting your subconscious flow. You visualize every day, so don't say that you can't do it – yes, you can!

Here's a visualization to help you make past-life connections:

Imagine you're in a forest.

Now really imagine you're in a forest!

Feel it, see it, sense it, smell it and hear it.

Ahead of you there's a pathway. Follow it and enjoy the feeling of peace and calm you get from being in the forest.

As you move along the path you begin to see a clearing ahead of you, a well-tended area with flowers and a circular lawn, perfect in every detail.

At one end there's an oak tree, the largest you have ever seen, and at the base of that tree is an oak door.

For now, just make your way to the centre of the lawn.

Stand in the centre of the lawn and wait until a bell rings. It's a great bell and its sound reverberates through the air.

The door beneath the tree opens and through it comes a procession of people in all sorts of clothing from all sorts of times and places. Some of them you may recognize straight away and others you may not know right now.

Let them form a circle around you and then look into their eyes.

Look into their eyes until you find the person you're looking for or someone you want to know more about.

When you do, touch them on the shoulder and watch as everyone else leaves you alone and goes back into the tree.

When you're alone with them, look into their eyes again and wait – wait for the pictures of your shared life or lives to come to you. You may hear them, see them or experience a combination of both, it really doesn't matter how you do it, just allow the information to flow.

When you're ready, say your goodbyes and let them return to the tree, closing the door behind them.

Now make your way out of the clearing and into the forest, walking back along the path you came in.

As you walk along the path, let the image fade and bring your awareness back into the room you're in.

Wiggle your fingers and toes and open your eyes. Write down your experience and be honest with yourself. Write down what could make things easier between you both, including what you need to do as well as what may need to be addressed between you.

Eat and drink – tea and cake it is, then!

Remember visualization and meditation are powerful tools, but they must be used with a purpose in mind. Sitting waiting for something to happen during meditation usually results in sleep! If you meditate on a word like 'peace', or perhaps 'harmony', that's what you invite in, so it doesn't have to be difficult to find a reason to meditate. All I am saying is don't just sit down and see what comes to you – have a reason!

While I'm on the subject, here are a few more guidelines for you.

General Guidelines for Meditation

Embrace your meditation with no expectations, as what's right for you will come your way, and even when using guided visualizations that you have done many times before, don't worry about seeing something other than what you normally see. Everything has value.

Here are a few things to bear in mind.

Try not to:

○   Force something to happen.

○   Over-analyse during the meditation.

O   Make your mind blank. If you keep a blank mind you will learn nothing!

O   Put too much emphasis on 'doing it right'. Just relax and enjoy the experience.

O   Meditate on a completely empty stomach. If you're hungry, have a little something to eat beforehand – not a roast dinner, obviously!

O   Meditate yourself to sleep. You may nod off wide open and have some funky dreams!

Do try to:

O   Find a quiet, comfortable place to meditate. You can sit in a chair, on the bed, on the floor – anywhere that's comfortable. It's not necessary to sit cross-legged.

O   When you sit to meditate, sit comfortably, with your spine reasonably straight. This allows the energy to flow freely, which is an important aspect of meditation.

O   Leaning against a chair back, a wall, headboard, etc. is perfectly all right. If, for physical reasons, you can't sit up, lie flat on your back.

○ Place your hands in any position that is comfortable, I find palms up on my legs is the best way for me.

○ Eliminate as many potential distractions as possible, but don't worry about those things that you cannot control.

○ If it doesn't go against your beliefs, call on your guides, angels or helpers before you begin.

Of course, you can also light candles, ring bells, do the hokey-cokey and turn around if it helps – the secret is to make your meditation routine your own.

There's much more on meditation and visualization in *David Wells' Complete Guide to Developing Your Psychic Skills.*

And Finally...

Past-life regression is and will remain a favourite of mine. It gives you so much more than you think and, as in Lorna's case, there's always something that has a knock-on effect in this life. So when someone suggests to you that they have enough problems in this life without dealing with issues from the past, you can enlighten them!

Chapter 7

Catherine's Story

The occasional seminar or the odd weekend away doing something you love is a great way to encourage your spiritual growth. Every time you make the effort, you gain more knowledge, but sometimes – in fact more than sometimes – it's about the people you meet along the way.

Catherine came to a weekend of workshops I was taking part in. She and her partner Peter arrived late and a little flustered after a very long journey. When you're with a group, that does make you stand out and I felt their energy as soon as they walked into the room. It wasn't as sparkly as some – in fact, I could feel some sadness there. It was nothing too great, but enough to make me want to get to them as soon as I could to see how they were doing.

After dinner there was the obligatory 'get to know you' quiz – you know, the kind of ice-breaker which, no matter what you think about this sort of thing, actually works! Beforehand I was heading to the bar when I saw Catherine and Peter sitting on their own, so I said hello and started a conversation.

Catherine told me a story that pulled at my heart strings. Her son Brandon had been brain damaged by her ex-husband, his biological father, shaking him violently at 12 weeks old. As she explained in an e-mail she sent after the weekend, he was older now but still 'unable to communicate verbally other than to babble, with only the odd word being recognizable' and unable to walk. I was keen to help her and asked if it would be possible to visit her to do some work with Brandon to see if I could communicate with him through his subconscious mind and maybe teach Catherine and Peter to communicate with him in the same way. A date was made and a visit organized.

I wasn't sure exactly how I was going to help Catherine and her family, but remembering that wasn't for me to worry about right now, I set off, knowing that if I could help her reach Brandon on a psychic level there would some changes on the physical level too. If we affect the psychic and emotional bodies, the change has to become part of the physical at some point, something that is not only part of the Qabalah but is supported by many other forms of teaching too.

I knew from my own experience that meditating or doing creative visualization could make a huge difference to the way certain scenarios went. For example, if I was going into a meeting I knew was going to be awkward, I would see myself at that meeting doing very well, getting things moving in the direction I wanted and ending up with the right result. By putting yourself in such a scenario in a visualization, you tell your physical self that you have been here before and you can do this, you can have what you want, as described in Chapter 3.

It's especially useful to do this when emotions are running high. We all know it's never easy when you have something to say to those you love, for instance, or perhaps those you have loved. 'I just want to be friends,' 'It's not you, it's me,' 'I love you but not that way...' – heard them all in my time and sometimes said them too! We often get ourselves worked up about a situation like that and in doing so we wind the energy around the situation up with it, adding another layer of worry and charging the air with the electrical energy of confrontation, but what if we were to just step back and think about it for a few minutes?

I had split up with a partner of many years and I knew it would be difficult to meet again, even loud and angry. I was determined that shouldn't happen and fortunately in my Qabalistic studies we had been taught that energy was everything (remember that secret?) and that we could have a say in how that energy was used. So, before driving to the meeting, I imagined my ex, starting with the eyes and letting the face build and then the neck and shoulders and then the rest of the body, and I saw them smiling, laughing and happy, and then I surrounded them in pink light. I just put them in a bubble of pure pink light and filled it with love and left them smiling and happy. It was then that I noticed a silver thread that seemed to come from my heart to theirs and along it was being transmitted love.

I came out of my meditation and started the physical journey to meet my ex.

The meeting was horrible – there was shouting and crying and things being thrown around the room and at one point a lovely chocolate cake was thrown at the wall.

Not really!

It was a very easy transition from ex to best friend, we still are the very best of friends and rather than being the end it could have been it was a fresh new beginning, but here's the thing: it was my intention to make things good between us, it was my desire that things were calm at the meeting and remained that way, and it was my wish that we remained buddies. If I had chosen to have a calm meeting and then never see them again that would have been fine too, but it was intention that made all the difference. And the starting point was the meditation.

So be clear about what you want when you employ your psychic self, be sure what the outcome will be and what the benefits to you will be and above all never, ever use energy shifting for anything other than good. It will bite you on the bottom if you do. So there.

The secret to using your psychic gifts is to use them. Daily.

Home Visit

I arrived at Catherine and Peter's home and rang the bell. Catherine answered and I was shown into the lounge, where I met Brandon for the first time. When I saw him I almost cried, not because this beautiful child couldn't walk or talk or communicate in any way that I could see, but because of the simplicity of his soul. He was truly a bundle of love, and love in its purest form can knock over the energy of even the most practised sensitive!

He made his way over to say hello and sat there staring at my hair! I know it can be a little choppy on occasions, but Catherine said he was always fascinated by people's hair. Could it be that he was seeing the energy from my crown chakra? There was a lot more going on with Brandon than was immediately obvious.

After speaking to Catherine and Peter, I decided that I would teach Catherine a technique to enable her to visit Brandon on another level, to talk to him in the astral worlds – a place where their souls rather than their physical bodies would be having the conversation. Peter took Brandon to his own room whilst Catherine and I got settled. It wasn't necessary for Brandon to be in the room physically.

The Meditation

I had asked and asked about this one, and my intuition, coupled with a lot of help from my guides, suggested I take Catherine to a place on the Qabalistic Tree of Life (don't worry, I'll explain in Chapter 9) called Tiphareth. This is the point of balance and of healing and a place I personally feel very comfortable in. It's also a place where children play in the garden, which seemed appropriate to the situation.

I am aware of the tree's power, so I decided to take Catherine into one of the ante-rooms away from the main temple, somewhere she could feel the energy but not be blown away by it! It's important to know what's right for a situation. Going beyond those limits could have exhausted her!

Catherine made herself comfortable and we began by breathing slowly and deliberately and then continued with this visualization:

See yourself in a forest. Remember to build it around you and to use all your senses to see, hear, feel, taste and touch it.

Now see a gate, a small white wooden gate with a golden path behind it, a path you want to follow. Follow it and in time, in your own time, you will see a hill on your left. This hill is covered in lush green grass and its smell fills your nostrils.

Ahead of you is a white marble temple, a church-like building with huge golden doors that swing open as you approach. You're directed to a side room.

Walk in and see a small church that's all white – white pews, white altar, white walls, white floor, all white marble – and the place breathes as if alive, giving off peace and tranquillity.

In the distance you can hear a choir, but you can't see it. To your left you see a door. It's surrounded by light and above it is a name: Brandon. Stand in front of the door and wait.

If he appears, have your conversation, ask what you need to ask and spend time with your beautiful son.

When it's time to leave, see the door close properly behind you and walk out of the cathedral.

Follow your path and go back through the white door, and as you walk through your forest, let it fade and bring yourself back into your own physical surroundings.

Have a cup of tea and a biscuit!

And write down your experiences.

Catherine was tearful, as you can imagine, but as we talked I could see a light go on in her, there was a lightening if you like, a look that said, 'I am at peace.' I was delighted to have helped, even if only for that moment in time, and we said our goodbyes.

Follow Up

I contacted Catherine some time later to thank her for the wonderful experience. I felt truly blessed to have been part of it. This is an extract from what she wrote in response:

I felt so at peace with the world when you left and that feeling stayed with me all day. Brandon has not been clingier, but there is a definite difference in his behaviour. He was much more content all of yesterday and very smiley, even at bedtime, so thank you once again.

So we had taken a small step forward and I was happy that Catherine had found some peace. I sent her a copy of the visualization so that she could do it at home whenever she felt the need.

She responded by telling me that since our meeting Brandon had become a lot more vocal, not saying actual words but making more distinguishable sounds, and he had become a lot closer to her, asking for cuddles and reaching out, which he hadn't done much of before.

It's important to note here that this has nothing to do with me other than the fact that I showed the way – this is pure spirit doing what it does when you take the time and effort to make the connection.

Sometime later Catherine had the opportunity to do some work on her own, something that was important for her. I'll let her relate it in her own words:

I have tried the meditation privately a couple of times and I have noticed significant changes in my son's behaviour, especially towards me.

He has become much more affectionate with me and has started to gesture to me that he wants affection in the form of cuddles and kisses without my needing to ask for them.

He has also become a lot calmer and has expressed this both to myself and Pete and also in the way he handles his toys, e.g. he has a lot of cuddly toys but has some soft Rottweiler puppy toys that originally belonged to Peter that he has always liked but his main act with these used to be to pick them up and shake them and throw them about, whereas now he picks them up and strokes them, and when he does this he says, 'Awwwh, awwwh,' and cuddles them.

He can also be heard to make this noise a lot when he is either showing us affection or requesting it from us.

I believe now that his prior actions may have been something to do with what his memory holds from the wrongful behaviour that his soul witnessed.

He has also become very vocal since the meditation, making many more sounds, and the words he was able to say originally are much more defined.

He is also a lot more alert to his sensitive side and frequently will try to communicate with someone he sees in the house. I like to think that this is his great-grandfather, as a lot of the signs this person gives me point towards him. After you said that the 'male presence' in the house loved fish and chips, I checked with my mum and she told me that my grandfather used to send her to the chip shop for a portion of fish and chips for him many times and he very rarely ordered any other meal for himself.

I feel that the meditation has also helped me in my journey on this Earth. I have always felt ... that I was placed here to nurture and care for people and I feel that's possibly why Brandon's dad, my ex-husband, hurt Brandon's physical being so badly and left his beautiful soul entrapped inside his body. Before, I felt as though I had failed him. I also felt that I had failed myself, because I was his protector, his carer, his leader and most important of all his mother, and I had let him down.

It has taken me a long time to come to terms with the things that have happened and I feel that as a result of this my bond with this beautiful boy who I am so proud to call my son has suffered.

When we did the meditation the first time and I was standing there looking at my son with his golden hair and beautiful blue eyes standing in front of me unaided, surrounded by the most angelic light I have ever been privileged to witness, my heart was full of mixed emotions – sadness for what would never be and the things he would never experience, joy for the vision I was beholding, guilt for the helplessness I had been feeling when he had been so determined and had overcome so much, and fear of hearing the answers I had anticipated to my questions, of which I had so many.

Tears of great joy rolled down my face when for the first time I heard my son speak to me... He asked me not to cry and said that he was happy in his life. He told me that he understood that I hadn't been able to help him at the time and that I had done everything I could to help him since.

I then asked him if he blamed me for what had happened to him, to which he replied, 'No, Mummy, I love you.' I asked him if he loved his daddy Pete, to which he replied, 'Of course, he's my daddy.' I knew then that he had accepted our family set-up and that the bond between him and his step-dad had progressed to a strong natural bond that only a father and his son could share.

I did not ask him any questions about his biological father as I did not want to use this special time to dredge up painful memories.

With regard to his change in behaviour, I think this is partly due to his being able to make me understand in our sessions what it is he is trying to convey to me at certain times and also that we have both, I feel, finally been able to let go of the past and just concentrate on our future together.

Personally I think that I now don't emit the negative energy that I used to when I was with him because I no longer dwell on what he can't have and instead I focus on how much joy he actually brings to my life and how blessed I am to have him in it.

I used to ask why if God existed would he let this happen to my innocent little boy and now I see that God cannot stop all things from happening, he just cannot be everywhere at once and we have to support each other, but he stepped in when he could and stopped me losing my son altogether, as well as giving him the courage, the energy and the determination to overcome all obstacles, no matter how great, and for this I am truly thankful.

Pause for a second, dwell on the love this woman has for her son and he for her and think about all those you love and how fortunate we all are.

Is it necessary to attempt to make sense of it all? We could ponder on why Brandon chose this path, if indeed you think he did choose it, why his mum is his mum in this incarnation and whether soul age has anything do with it; it could go on forever and get you no closer to the purity of the love this family shares.

Brandon and family will be receiving a visit from me when I pass by their part of the country, which I hope will be soon and often.

Chapter 8

Iona's Journey

People often ask me about healing – what's the secret to healing yourself and others? It's important to realize that wounds can be many and varied. They could come from a past life, or a current situation, or perhaps your own failure to recognize that you're not dealing with an emotional issue and so having it manifest as a disease – dis-ease. There are many theories and some fantastic books on the subject, but in principle if the etheric or spiritual body creates the illness, it's not a giant leap to assume it can also heal it.

I was considering how best to express my thoughts on healing to you when I met Iona. She and her husband, Paul, came to a workshop on psychic development. She was very interested in the subject and wanted to find out more about herself and how to develop her abilities. At lunchtime she and her husband walked back with me to the conference room and it was clear she was struggling with the walk and it was a real effort for her to use the stairs, but she impressed me by using them rather than taking the lift.

After the workshop, I kept thinking about her and the way she was trying so hard even though she clearly wasn't well. I admire people who persevere, people who find the strength to keep going and to challenge themselves along the way.

Later Iona e-mailed to tell me that since the workshop she had had the courage to resign from her career as she needed to focus on her health.

I had considered putting my own theories on healing to the test and Iona kept coming into my mind over and over again. Eventually I found the time to sit down and think about what to do, to ask my guides for their advice and to listen to my intuition. It was clear I had a chance to make a difference with Iona, and more importantly, I wanted to.

How to begin?

I am not a trained healer, at least not a trained spiritual healer. I know many of them, and some amazing ones at that, but I haven't worked for or been trained by any organization such as the National Federation of Spiritual Healers (NFSH) which does some wonderful work and even has some trained professionals working in NHS hospitals (and about time too)!

I was trained in Reiki, a Japanese healing technique, but decided not to proceed from level two to master. To be honest, that was a decision taken mainly because I couldn't get along with the word 'master'. I am aware that not everyone shares my concerns and that's fine, but I just can't use the word when it's associated with a spiritual practice as it smacks of superiority for me and if there is one thing I am resolute about it's that we are all equal.

That aside, all healing techniques seem to work on energy, and if everything is made of energy then we should be able to manipulate it and send it where we want with the power of intention. It's *intention* that matters. Any healing technique will surely fail if the person transmitting it isn't directing it appropriately, which is why the golden rule is always to be healthy yourself before you attempt to heal another.

I wanted to test these beliefs, to challenge my own thoughts on how the human body is affected by the energy from both inside and outside the physical shell, and I also wanted to do the best I could for Iona.

I e-mailed her and asked her if she would agree to my sending her some remote healing. In other words, I wouldn't be able to be with her but would attempt to send healing energy from a distance. To make things easier I would do it at 6 p.m. UK time wherever I was in the world. She agreed.

Scanning

I was determined to follow my own intuition and purposely stayed away from reading any books on healing techniques. Surely if energy was universal it would be possible to direct it using my own method, very simply seeing it moving towards Iona and allowing it to go where it was needed.

I asked Iona to sit somewhere she felt comfortable, to make sure telephones were off and that she was as relaxed as she could be. Then I did the same from my home and imagined her standing in front of me. I was aware of her aura and scanned it to find any holes or odd areas I could concentrate on. I surrounded her in pink light and was aware of some dark spaces on her right shoulder, the right side of her head and her left thigh and hip. I pushed light into these areas and kept pushing until I felt the aura was complete again. I was very conscious of making sure the energy was moving all the time, as it's my belief it must keep moving around and in and out – in from the crown and out through the feet and hands.

The next day I was away travelling, but I took time out to make sure I tuned in and sent Iona healing. We should be able to do all our psychic work wherever we are. I love my crystals and candles, but I am aware that magic can happen whether you're sitting in your most sacred space or at a service station on the M6. It's always preferable to be in your ideal spot, but don't let that limit your capacity to make a difference.

I kept up the absent healing for a week and afterwards Iona wrote to me to tell me what she had experienced:

I have very positive feedback from the healing both on a physical level and a spiritual level.

You are spot on with the right shoulder and right side of my head. I had a whiplash injury three years ago and suffer greatly with pain in those areas. Again, you are right with the thigh and hip – again the aftermath of the accident. I am quite

*troublesome really! But you are completely right. I
am truly amazed.*

*I have documented each day's findings in a journal
some 20 pages long and feel that writing everything
down has helped with the healing. I would love you
to read my journal because I think it would give
you a better indication of how you have helped me.
Would it be possible for me to send it to you?*

Of course it would. I found it very interesting
reading. Here are some extracts:

Monday 6th April

6 p.m. *Ten minutes' absent healing. I relax, lie down and
try to free my mind and focus on David. I have David's
book to my left hand.*

*I feel a cool sensation in the lower half of my body and
tingles in my left hand.*

*I feel as if David is in a very light room, a bright room
with lots of light. I feel relaxed and happy.*

Approximately 10 p.m. *I feel a 'cool' or 'cooling'
sensation at the back of my neck – quite a nice feeling. My
neck has been the root cause of much of my pain and has
caused me much discomfort since I was in a car accident
three years ago and sustained a whiplash injury.*

Tuesday 7ᵗʰ April

I have had a really good night's sleep and have been dreaming. I cannot quite remember the dream, other than it being a nice experience. A really good night's sleep is a rarity for me.

I feel still quite tired, a feeling that is a large part of my life due to the ME condition that I have.

I do feel mentally calm, serene and quite spiritual, however the fatigue is quite extraordinary and overwhelming.

***6 p.m.** Again I lie down with David's book under my left hand.*

This time I feel that David isn't in the same place. Somewhere different from yesterday? Not sure where.

The experience is also different. This time I feel heat coming from my left hand. Again I feel totally relaxed.

***9 p.m.** Again, once I am able to relax and sit down, I experience a cooling sensation at the back of my neck in much the same way that I did the previous evening – a subtle feeling, but nice and reassuring.*

SUMMARY
Overall today, I can honestly say that I have felt different, more subdued, more relaxed. The tiredness has been

incredible. I have found it difficult to do anything of substance. It is as if my body is telling me to stop what I am doing and free my mind of any worry or stress. Usually I worry about things, but today has been different.

Wednesday 8ᵗʰ April
I have had another good night's sleep.

I usually feel quite weak both mentally and physically, but after the two days' attunement, my mind feels stronger.

6 p.m. *Again I have David's book under my left hand and I feel electricity or tingling coming from my left hand.*

I can feel tingling sensations tonight on my upper body, particularly around my head and neck region.

I am inclined to smile and feel warm inside. I am enjoying the moment and feel good about myself.

9 p.m. *On relaxing I can feel a coolness around my neck and shoulders – exactly the same sensation as on the previous two nights. It feels good. The tightness I have in the muscles is much calmer.*

I feel extremely relaxed and am enjoying the feeling of lying on the sofa.

SYNOPSIS
Today has been a quiet day but a good day for reflection and thought. I am positive that David's healing energy is truly helping me to relax and reflect. I feel that the fatigue is not a negative facet and that I really do need the rest to recuperate. I have been in pain for quite some time now.

Thursday 9th April
8 a.m. I slept really well last night. I dreamed but I cannot remember the dream, just fragments of it. My sleep pattern is usually very poor.

2.30 p.m. I saw a flyer for an art class earlier and thought it would be a good move for me, so I telephoned the lady involved. I felt inspired by what she told me. She was very friendly and encouraging and I decided to go along. Taking action is creation in itself. I am so pleased I have finally made a decision and am getting involved with something creative.

5.30 p.m. Tune in with David. I feel relaxed and have his book under my left hand once more. I have tingles in my left hand. David signed this book at the workshop.

Tonight I feel that David is in a different place from the previous two nights. I think of him and ask for his energy to heal me. What I would do to feel 100 per cent again.

I feel coolness on the upper half of my body – a nice sensation, soothing and caressing. I feel so very tired this evening. Could it be that toxins are being released?

7.30 p.m. *As on the previous nights following David's healing I have a cooling sensation at the back of my neck. It is a relief to me.*

10 p.m. *The cooling sensation continues. It is bliss and I am still lying on the sofa, tired but elated.*

SUMMARY
Of all the days, this has been my most fatigued, but the pain element of my illness is truly better. I do not feel stressed; I am happy and feel extremely positive.

Friday 10th April
8 a.m. *Awaken. It is Good Friday today and a day of rest. I feel pretty good and relaxed. The fatigue is OK. Slept pretty well.*

My neck feels relaxed. It is a real tonic for it to be like this. It hasn't been like this for two years!

6 p.m. *Tune in with David. I have his book under my left hand again and immediately I can feel tingles in my left hand and tonight also my right hand. I visualize David sending me healing energy. Cannot tell where he is tonight, difficult to say.*

I feel relaxed and soothed. I feel a wave of calmness.

SUMMARY
I have had a really good day. I have felt very relaxed, incredibly spiritual and in tune with my environment.

The tension is subsiding in my neck and although the fatigue never wanes, I find it tolerable.

Saturday 11th April
My neck muscles feel free. Wow! Usually I am as stiff as a poker. I feel happy and relaxed and again very spiritual. The fatigue is tolerable.

6 p.m. This time I have David's book under my right hand. I feel tingling predominately in my right hand but also in my left hand. I have flashes of light in front of my eyes, different colours. I lie still and I feel as if I am floating. I find the experience uplifting and moving. It is one of pure elation. I see visions of mountains, faraway places and places of tranquillity.

6.45 p.m. Relaxing on the sofa, I feel like dropping off to sleep. The muscles in my neck feel relaxed and cool. And, as on the previous nights, I have a cooling sensation around my neck as if magic is being performed there, as if hands are caressing my neck and healing me.

10.30 p.m. *An early night, but needed, as tiredness is setting in, but a nice tiredness, not the usual tiredness that goes with my illness. A tiredness that welcomes sleep.*

SUMMARY
A day of pure joy and beauty. I have enjoyed this day so much. The tension has lifted from my body. My fatigue is still there but I know that one day the medical profession will find a cure and until then I have the love of everyone I know to carry me through it.

My neck feels better too.

Sunday 12th April
The last day of David's healing.

8 a.m. *We wake up to the morning sunshine peeping through the curtains. It is going to be a beautiful day. I feel so good that I could cry. My neck muscles feel relaxed, not stiff and tense, and I have had a good night's sleep. I feel happy and alive.*

2 p.m. *My muscles feel oiled and flexible. I feel really good. I attempt to polish a cupboard. I am surprised by my energy and enthusiasm.*

6 p.m. *I link in with David for the final healing. I lie down and relax and open my mind. I have David's book under my left hand and a quartz crystal in my right. I feel* tingling in my left hand and also in my right. Tonight, for the first time, I have a feeling of extreme heat in my left foot, the site of a previous injury which can be troublesome. It is a healing and warming sensation and feels wonderful. I feel very relaxed and trouble-free. I think in future it would be good for me to incorporate a period of self-soothing/meditation on a daily basis in order to continue the good work David has commenced.

9.30 p.m. On retiring to the lounge I have the healing sensation in my neck muscles once more. It makes me feel very relaxed and I feel immense joy.

SUMMARY
I feel that the week of healing has been very successful. I think that there has been an improvement daily, not only in my physical symptoms but also my mental/spiritual awareness. My neck is more relaxed and free and my muscles are much more relaxed also. My mental wellbeing has also improved. I feel calmer and much more positive and am looking towards taking small steps towards self-improvement. I feel that there is a light at the end of the tunnel and I am using a spiritual torch to guide myself towards it.

Befriending like-minded people, attending workshops and above all remaining positive are the keys to my future. I have closed the door on one career and am looking forward to opening the door to another opportunity. I *am hoping to pursue a career in a healing or spiritual capacity and am asking my angels and guides to point me in the right direction.*

For Iona, the journey still continues, and I have put her on a healing list that I share with some incredible healers in Essex (*see* www.purespirithealingcentre. com *for more information*), but how can you help those around you, or yourself for that matter?

Energy

Remember the secret? It's all about energy...

Chakras

This Sanskrit word means 'wheel' and your chakras are literally that, wheels of energy that sit in your aura, or energetic body, the one that surrounds your physical one, the one that goes 'ouch' when you hear bad news, tingles when you feel love or just picks up on an odd atmosphere when you are in a haunted house! There are thousands of chakras on your body, 88,000 to be exact, but just for now we will concentrate on the main seven running from the base of your spine to your crown.

Place your hand over your heart, about 4 inches over it. What do you feel? Can you feel the flow of energy? Or perhaps it's just heat? Now move your hand to the right, away from your heart. Can you feel the boundaries of your chakra? If you can, consciously think about your chakra opening up and then see if you can get it to meet your hand.

Do the same with your crown, your throat, your belly button. What do you feel, where do you feel it the strongest and is there a direction to the energy, is the wheel spinning clockwise or anti-clockwise? The base chakra in males tends to rotate clockwise, females anti-clockwise, and they then alternate as you come up your body.

There are so many things that can be helped by this magical awareness. Take some time to research chakras in more depth and you will be amply rewarded.

Now what if you want to apply that knowledge to healing someone?

First of all, ask permission to send healing – it's only manners!

You must be feeling healthy yourself, as it's important you have some energy to direct. It also needs to be very positive energy, so if you're in a moody it's better to leave it until later.

If all that's sorted and you're ready to begin, try this:

Sit somewhere comfortable. Don't lie down – that usually ends up in sleep and that's not the purpose here.

Close your eyes and breathe in and out slowly. Breathe in on a count of four, hold it for two, breathe out for four and hold it for two, then breathe in again and repeat.

Relax.

See a ball of light above your head. Let it sparkle and shine and then let it form a rod of light right through your body, a rod of pure white light moving from your crown to your feet and flowing out of your feet and out of your hands as you charge your own aura, making it bigger, brighter and more beautiful!

Imagine now a ball of energy coming from your chest, from your heart chakra. See it as pink or green, whichever suits you. See it sparkling and shining, spinning in front of you perhaps.

Now imagine the person you wish to send healing to and begin to see their aura, the light surrounding them. If you can't see their aura, imagine them surrounded in pink light.

It's time now to see if you can pick out any holes in their aura. Make a note of where they are and give yourself a mental picture of that aura.

Now turn your attention back to the ball on your chest and see it move from you towards them. See it surrounding them and flowing into those holes. See their aura as a moving vibrant light repairing those holes with your healing energy. See your healing energy lifting their energy and increasing their light.

Use your intuition to find areas that need more work.

When you're ready, see the light withdrawing and coming back to you.

Let it flow upwards and out into the universe to be healed and used wherever higher forces deem necessary.

Allow your own aura to return to its usual resting size. This will happen naturally, but interestingly it's likely to be greater than when you started!

Begin to return to your surroundings. Bring yourself back and open your eyes.

Write down your impressions.

Remember to have a cup of tea and a biscuit, or better still a slice of chocolate fudge cake, anything that will help you ground your energy, in other words bring yourself back into your physical awareness.

If you wish to perform healing on yourself, scan your own aura and follow the rest of the healing as is.

Maintaining a Healthy Aura

Here's another wonderful technique that will boost your own aura no end! I'll ask you to do this every day for two weeks. Persevere – it's worth the effort!

Take a deep breath.

Hold it for six seconds and release it.

Repeat.

Tense your feet and relax.

Tense your calves and relax.

Tense your thighs and relax.

Tense your stomach muscles and relax.

Tense your arms and relax.

Tense your shoulders and relax.

Tense your neck and relax.

Screw your face up and laugh!

Visualize a white light above your head, a brilliant white light.

See that light move down the front of your body, leaving a trail of brilliant white light like a ribbon.

Let it move under your feet and up your back, returning to its starting point above your head.

Repeat this five times.

Now see the light moving down your left shoulder, down the side of your body, under your feet and back up your right side to the starting point above your head.

Repeat five times.

Imagine a light at your left foot. See it move to your right foot and then let it come around your body in a spiral movement, wrapping you in a ribbon of white light, sealing your aura in shining white light.

Let it come all the way up to your crown and unite it with the ball of light above your head, encasing you in that brilliant white light.

Do this every day for two weeks until it becomes automatic, until all you have to do is think, 'Interwoven light,' and it's there.

Look after Yourself...

It's all too easy to want to help others all of the time, but I am moved to remind you that your own energy is important and if you overdo things you will just exhaust yourself. If you feel worn out, if you feel tired, if you feel as if you have had every ounce of your energy drained, you're overdoing it.

Limit yourself to what you feel comfortable with and no matter how much you're tempted to do more and more, stay away from it if you can barely make yourself a mug of hot chocolate in the evening – a good test!

Chapter 9

Qabalah

am often asked, 'How do you know these sorts of things?' Of course, a lot of it is through experience and experiences, but there had to be a framework for it all to hang on and for me that was the Qabalah. This is clearly one of the biggest secrets I can give you, the system that opened all the doors to the spiritual realms for me, and I am happy to share what I know of this incredible tool.

Study of the Qabalah in my opinion never ends, there's always some new way to look at things. Here's what my own teacher, Jenni Shell, says about it:

There are many disagreements about the Qabalah, even down to the spelling of the name. It's better known as Kabbalah or Cabala, but if we make the effort we will find many more variations, each purporting to be right!

Some say the subject only came into being in the Middle Ages while others suggest that it has been studied for thousands of years. However, most would agree that it is of Jewish origin.

The Qabalah cannot be classed as a religion in any sense, although it successfully encompasses the values of all of them. However, it has been known as the 'mystical interpretation of the Old Testament' and those who study it say it gives many explanations of biblical statements and resolves apparent contradictions that have sometimes confused understanding. Although it is based on Jewish tradition, many of non-Jewish persuasion study the subject.

The study of the Qabalah is the examination of the individual on every level – from the physical self to the higher spiritual entity – and this is just one aspect of it, for it also encompasses a spectrum of infinite possibilities, including the idea of other worlds, the magical power of number and language, and universal concepts that move us closer to understanding our origins and destiny.

The principal tool of examination is what is known as the Tree of Life – a diagram of 10 circles (Sephiroth), linked together by lines (paths), which make it strangely resemble DNA. It relates not only to the 10 aspects of the human psyche but also, amongst many other things, to the 10 Cosmic Laws of Creation and the 10 Faces of the

Creator, of which we are but a reflection. In very simplistic terms, the Tree of Life can be likened to a 'reference map' of 10 Temples of Light through which the disciple may travel on the road to self-discovery, using the 22 paths which link one temple to another.

There are many arguments as to what the Qabalah is or is not, and indeed the right ways of accessing it. However, the Tree of Life is so versatile it encompasses all things for all people, and therein lies its infinite value, for whether we are of a certain religious persuasion, an atheist, agnostic, materialist, philosopher, psychologist, scientist or simply querent, it acknowledges such variety of opinion yet opens doorways of new perception that help us to really know and understand where we come from, what we believe in and above all why we do so.

The key words for the Qabalah are 'Know Thyself.' This may seem a simple statement, and indeed it is, yet those who study it find themselves not only in a never-ending field of self-discovery, but also discovery of the world and universe around them.

Whatever way we look at it, from the simplistic to the complex, the Qabalah responds to the level of our personal understanding, is open to challenge and holds many answers that have hitherto defied explanation. By studying the Tree of Life we get in touch with just one aspect of this remarkable subject, but perhaps this is the *most important area, for it is directly associated with ourselves in the personal sense, as well as part of human evolution.*

The Qabalah, therefore, is arguably not *a religion but more a* philosophy *and, although it does not purport to make life easier, it* does *help us ensure that we can make it much better. Its value is in the use of the Tree of Life as a psychological 'tool' and its study can be likened to taking a degree in life.*

Taken from www.orderofthewhitelion.com

I studied with Jenni for almost 12 years and whilst that may sound like a very long time it wasn't as if there was a test at the end, the tests were all the way through it, in fact, and to be fair I was the one doing the testing rather than being tested. For me, the Qabalah is magical because it presents itself in our everyday life, reminding us that our spiritual self is integrated with our physical, not separate, and not something we can attend to once a week and then be free for the rest of the time to create havoc as long as one day we say sorry!

When I decided to write this chapter I was determined to do so from my heart, without reference books and from my own experiences, to let it flow from me to you in the way the 'Q', as I affectionately call it, was meant to be passed on – a spoken tradition passed from my soul to yours.

So Where Did It Come From?

Tradition says the Qabalah was handed to humanity by an angel. Some say it was the archangel Michael, some say Raphael, but most agree it was down to angelic forces and no matter if you study the 'Q' or the Kaballah or Cabala, it was given to the Jewish people as a way to live their lives on Earth and then was spread through word of mouth to other lands and other cultures.

It's not a religion, it's not a cult and it most definitely isn't dogmatic in any way, shape or form.

It has had its share of famous names attached to it, or allegedly attached to it, names like Shakespeare, Keats, Jung, Galileo, Blake, Newton and Einstein for example, none of whom you may notice sought fame for fame's sake and all of whom are famous for their contributions to humankind rather than their own personalities. Madonna is of course well known for her involvement with Kaballah. This isn't the same as the version I study. Mine appears to be more experiential and less reliant on things like red string and expensive bottled water. There are no oughts or shoulds about it, there are only suggestions and personal creativity, which is why I love it so much. It has set me free.

What Does It Do?

The 'Q' is often referred to as the Western Mystic Tradition and when I am asked for a label to describe what I do, I often say I am a modern mystic rather than an astrologer, psychic or any other one of those tags, but sadly that's a little too much for most. Then I smile and remind myself it's not about labels, others' thoughts or what they attract, it's about how *I* feel about myself and that's one of the lessons the 'Q' taught me very early on.

Gradually it showed me just what was and wasn't important, what my own strengths were and where I could improve, who was and wasn't good for me and how to recognize it in the future, and how the universal laws worked. One day I will write out the whole course for you in language that isn't as off-putting as that of most books on it. For now let's take a whistle-stop tour to unveil just a few so-called secrets about it. But remember, a secret is only a fact you have to look a little harder to find – nothing is truly secret if someone knows about it!

The Tree of Life

The central symbol of the Qabalah, the Tree of Life, works on the principle that our subconscious thinks in pictures, so when you attach experiences and events to symbols, you can draw them to you by the use of the appropriate symbol. An easy way to think of this is to imagine a picture of somewhere you were really happy. See it and step into it and you become happy, do you not? It makes you smile. Now imagine a time you weren't so happy and you may feel glum – enough of that! Back to happy land!

Let's see the Tree of Life (overleaf):

You will see there are 10 Sephiroth, pronounced 'sef-roth', spheres which are represented by the planets. There is also a hidden one, but that's for the other book perhaps. For now there are 10 and they represent the journey of manifestation, no matter whether that's the manifestation of a soul or an idea.

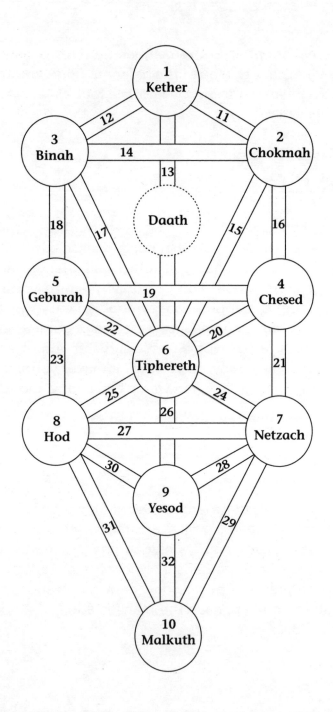

The paths between the Sephiroth are represented by the Major Arcana of the Tarot. That's again for another time. For now let's look at those Sephiroth.

If you begin at the top:

○   *Kether*, the planet Neptune, is pure nothing, no thought, just an energy, and is attached to the principle of God, the most complicated and yet simplest energy you can have, the source, and as such makes no judgements and sets no rules.

○   *Chockma*, pronounced 'hok-ma', the planet Uranus, is where we meet the spark of an idea. It's chaotic sometimes, but that first spark gets things moving. It's the 'Eureka!' moment, if you like.

○   *Binah*, pronounced 'bee-na', the planet Saturn, is where thought begins to take form and structures are added. Some order begins to form from the chaos. Perhaps a way to look at this is when you put bones and teeth onto your ideas, the skeleton forms.

○ *Chesed*, pronounced 'hess-ed', the planet
  Jupiter, is where the idea begins to be
  discussed and mulled over. It's all about
  what goes where and what happens if this,
  that or the other happens – the planning
  stages.

○ *Geburah*, pronounced 'ge-boo-ra', the
  planet Mars, is where it's time to take
  action, and that's action against all the
  nonsense that could cause a plan to fail.
  This is the place where severe changes may
  be made to ensure success.

○ *Tiphareth*, pronounced 'tiff-a-reth', the
  Sun, is the centre of the Tree of Life, the
  point of balance, and it brings the passion
  and planning of our idea into being and
  reminds us to be like a child, to have no
  expectations and a lot of excitement!

○ *Netzach*, pronounces 'net-sack', the
  planet Venus, is where we look at those
  very human things, our feelings and our
  instincts. It's where we react and just *know*
  what to do. This is the realm of beauty and
  it's here that the pretty bits of the plan are
  put together.

○ *Hod*, the planet Mercury, brings you to the point where now you have feelings you have to have thoughts, and as thoughts and feelings sit opposite each other you can see why you sometimes change your attitude or change how you feel or vice versa. Conscious thoughts are to the fore here and communication is the job of Hod.

○ *Yesod*, the Moon, is the realm of your intuition as opposed to your instinct. They are very different things. Your intuition involves your memory, and how things have been in the past has an effect on how you will find them in the future. Past-life memories reside in Yesod.

○ *Malkuth*, pronounced 'mal-kooth' and sometimes 'mal-coot' (it's fine either way), is Planet Earth – your final destination. Your idea is concrete and is actually happening, be that a new life, a new way of working or finally getting a holiday booked!

When you know the symbols you begin to understand where you are in any process you're going through, from work to your personal life, and when you know where you are on the map, you know how to get to your destination.

It's important to note that no one Sephiroth or path can work on its own, they are all linked and all need their neighbours in order for us to move ahead smoothly. For example, where would you be if all your ideas were uncontrolled or unrefined? You would dash off doing a million things when you really only needed to do a few.

Personal Links

We all have a personal Sephira (that's the singular of Sephiroth), we have one connected to our soul and one to our spiritual self. The latter are only really found by working on the tree, but our personal or personality Sephira can be found by simply looking for the planet that rules our Sun sign. So:

O   *Aries*, you are ruled by Mars: Geburah.

This gives you your high energy levels and your tendency to cut away the nonsense and get right to the core of the matter, but beware you're not severe on occasions and eliminate what could later be useful.

O   *Taurus*, you are ruled by Venus: Netzach.

You're a touchy-feely type, enjoying life's pleasures wherever and whenever you can get them! Feelings are great as long as you balance them with rational thoughts; when you overdo it you get grumpy because you 'feel' too much. Attitude changes come from balance.

O   *Gemini*, you are ruled by Mercury: Hod.

You have the communication thing under your belt big time, and as Mercury is the communicator god you understand the need for talk, but talk can sometimes be cheap and you may need to put your prices up, Gemini. Do you really feel what you say?

O   *Cancer*, you are ruled by the Moon: Yesod.

The wonder of the Moon is in her reflective nature and you're often used as a mirror for the emotions of others and in doing so you also absorb their stuff. You're designed to remember and you love those melancholy moments, but don't dwell there so long you forget the here and now.

O   *Leo*, you are ruled by the Sun: Tiphareth.

Big, brash, bold and balanced? The first three perhaps, but being in the centre of the tree means you are tested on keeping your balance, which of course means you're knocked out of it frequently! The trick is to remember what's around you. *Everything* is around you. Use it.

O *Virgo*, you are ruled by Mercury: Hod.

Although Gemini also has this Sephira, you use it more with the written word and the scheduling that the organization of the left-hand column can bring. You're at the foot of that pillar and it's down to you to put the rules in place.

O *Libra*, you are ruled by Venus: Netzach.

Taurus, too, has this ruler, but for you it's more about appreciation of beauty. The way you see the world may sometimes be through rose-tinted spectacles – perfect if you live a rose-tinted life, but if you don't it's instinct you need to cultivate, the ability to know what to do and when. Trust that instinct.

O *Scorpio*, you are ruled by Mars and Pluto: Geburah and, as Pluto is attached to the hidden Sephira, Malkuth can also be your personality Sephira.

Awkward, you? Never. Joking aside, Scorpio, you can be both severe with your energy and very earthy, with nothing being out of bounds as far as your conversations go, and you're always the first to discuss life's bigger questions like death, sex and the mysteries of the occult, but remember to turn that interest into something you love doing – health care, astrology, burlesque dancing?

○ *Sagittarius*, you are ruled by Jupiter: Chesed.

You can be tempted, but can't we all? Yes, of course, but you may be tempted to go over the top. Holding some sort of balance between what you think you can do and what you can actually do is essential, and here's the tricky bit: you have to be able to do that without limiting your possibilities.

○ *Capricorn*, you are ruled by Saturn: Binah.

Putting in structure and form is natural for you and as you look at what needs to be done you see the way ahead pretty easily, but can you let others do their thing or do you want to do it all yourself? You may assume responsibility for everything and everyone, but are you actually responsible?

○ *Aquarius*, you are ruled by Uranus: Chockma.

The realms of the unexpected and unpredictable are your happiest places. Wherever there is chaos there is also excitement, and your unique nature thrives on it. That's all well and good, but remember that from chaos order will eventually come.

○   *Pisces*, you are ruled by Neptune: Netzach.

Without shape or form, this Sephira isn't an easy one to grasp – does that sound familiar? You're linked to the top of the tree, where ideas are puffs of wind and sparkly lights, so how do you make them anything other than dreams? There's your challenge: how do you bring them from way up there to way down here?

Meditations on the Tree of Life

If you have followed some of the visualizations in my other books you will know that I often start them in a forest, and the reason for that is now clear. If you start your journey from Malkuth, Earth, then a forest is the perfect place to remind you that you are on the physical plane.

The other realms of the tree will unfold through visualizations and practical work and at a pace that's right for you, but for now it's time to visit the only one I can take you to in this book. For the others you need a lot more preparation, but the truth is you already live in the first one, though seeing that is sometimes the hardest step of all.

So join me in the beauty that is Malkuth. Sit a while and remind yourself of your commitment to your plan, to your incarnation, and the way you have already come down the tree in your journey into incarnation and into the great adventure called life.

Make yourself comfortable.

Breathe deeply and with a good solid rhythm.

Imagine that you're in a forest. See it, feel it, taste it, hear it and smell it. Use all your senses.

Walk among the trees and feel your feet on the path you have chosen. Feel the damp earth and see the vibrancy of the colours in the forest.

An animal may come to greet you. If they do, acknowledge them and follow them. They will give you clues to parts of yourself you may need to develop. For example, if you see a fox you may have to be more cunning, while a dog suggests being a team player. Check out whatever creature comes your way!

Walk along the path until you come to a clearing and in that clearing you will see a well-tended lawn, a beautiful lawn with flowerbeds around it.

At the far end of the clearing you will see a magnificent oak tree, the largest you have ever seen in your life, but this is no ordinary oak tree. Its branches sparkle with light as if the leaves are made of crystals and jewels and it seems to have an aura around it. If you listen carefully, you may even hear it sing.

Your animal moves towards a large wooden door at the foot of the tree and waits for you. Catch up with it. It won't go in, but you can.

Push the door open and step into the tree. Let your eyes adjust to the dim light.

Underneath your feet there's a black-and-white tiled floor and on that floor are herbs – basil, lavender, rosemary, all sorts of herbs – and as you walk on them they release their fragrance.

Ahead of you, you will see a double-cubed altar, like two dice one of top of the other, one black, one white, and on top of them is a simple white cloth and on top of that burns a single blue flame. This is the flame of Earth. How brightly is it burning?

Ahead of you is a circular stained-glass window with the face of a man in it, the most beautiful face you have ever seen, with golden hair and sapphire-blue eyes.

To your right is a window with a pouncing lion in it. Red and gold illuminate this window.

Behind you is a window with an eagle flying into the eye of a golden sun.

And to your left there is a window that holds a black charging bull in a field of poppies.

Now look ahead of you again and as you become more accustomed to the light you will see two pillars. The one on the left is made of ebony and the one on the right is made of ivory.

Behind those pillars you will see three doors, one on the left, one in the centre and one on the right. They are for another time, not for now.

In the dim light you are aware of eyes watching you. The owners of the eyes are interested in you and happy that you are there. For now, just acknowledge that they are friends and sit in the temple contemplating why you have incarnated. That's a big question but perhaps has a very simple answer.

When you're ready, move back through the temple and out into the clearing where your animal will be waiting. They will be happy to see you and may even dance around you. If you feel like it, dance with them!

Move through the clearing and into your forest, following your path, and when you're ready, say goodbye to your animal guide.

Now let the forest fade away and bring your awareness back into the room.

Kettle on, biscuits out, pen and paper at the ready for those all-important notes.

There's more, much more, but that's for another time. I simply couldn't write this book, though, without acknowledging this incredible tool that can help guide you through this earthly experience that we are all having. I have to say, however, that the 'Q' isn't the only way and I am certainly not evangelical about it. I know it worked for me, but whatever attracts you is the right thing for you.

Chapter 10

Rising to the Challenge

It seems that every book I've written ends with another piece of the astrological jigsaw that makes you who you are – this one, then, is no different!

So what's the secret? Well, have you ever thought you're not exactly as your Sun sign would say you were? Maybe you're a Virgo but far from tidy. Perhaps you're a peaceful Libra with an outspoken and noisy side. Maybe you're Aries Rising?

'What's my Rising Sign?'

How do you know what's rising in your chart and what does it mean? Sometimes called the ascendant, your rising sign is what was coming over the eastern horizon at the time of your birth and so you have to know the time of your birth to find it out. It is the coloured glass people see you through, it's what you present to the world and it's even how you look. It gives you the starting point for your chart and from there each part of your chart falls into place.

Check the table to find out which sign was rising when you were born, and if it still seems out, look at the ones either side or, better still, consult an astrologer, who will cast your chart to the second you were born. (It's also worth checking which house system they use, as different systems may result in different ascendants.)

SUN SIGN	Aries	Taurus	Gemini	Cancer
4am–6am	Aries	Taurus	Gemini	Cancer
2am–4am	Pisces	Aries	Taurus	Gemini
12am–2am	Aquarius	Pisces	Aries	Taurus
10pm–12am	Capricorn	Aquarius	Piscesw	Aries
8pm–10pm	Sagitarius	Capricorn	Aquarius	Pisces
6pm–8pm	Scorpio	Sagitarius	Capricorn	Aquarius
4pm–6pm	Libra	Scorpio	Sagitarius	Capricorn
2pm–4pm	Virgo	Libra	Scorpio	Sagitarius
12pm–2pm	Leo	Virgo	Libra	Scorpio
10am–12pm	Cancer	Leo	Virgo	Libra
8am–10am	Gemini	Cancer	Leo	Virgo
6am–8am	Taurus	Gemini	Cancer	Leo

SUN SIGN	Leo	Virgo	Libra	Scorpio
4am–6am	Leo	Virgo	Libra	Scorpio
2am–4am	Cancer	Leo	Virgo	Libra
12am–2am	Gemini	Cancer	Leo	Virgo
10pm–12am	Taurus	Gemini	Cancer	Leo
8pm–10pm	Aries	Gemini	Gemini	Cancer
6pm–8pm	Pisces	Aries	Gemini	Gemini
4pm–6pm	Aquarius	Pisces	Aries	Gemini
2pm–4pm	Capricorn	Aquarius	Pisces	Aries
12pm–2pm	Sagitarius	Capricorn	Aquarius	Pisces
10am–12pm	Scorpio	Sagitarius	Capricorn	Aquarius
8am–10am	Libra	Scorpio	Sagitarius	Capricorn
6am–8am	Taurus	Libra	Scorpio	Sagitarius

SUN SIGN	*Sagitarius*	*Capricorn*	*Aquarius*	*Pisces*
4am–6am	Sagitarius	Capricorn	Aquarius	Pisces
2am–4am	Scorpio	Sagitarius	Capricorn	Aquarius
12am–2am	Libra	Scorpio	Sagitarius	Capricorn
10pm–12am	Virgo	Libra	Scorpio	Sagitarius
8pm–10pm	Leo	Virgo	Libra	Scorpio
6pm–8pm	Cancer	Leo	Virgo	Libra
4pm–6pm	Gemini	Cancer	Leo	Virgo
2pm–4pm	Taurus	Gemini	Cancer	Leo
12pm–2pm	Aries	Taurus	Gemini	Cancer
10am–12pm	Pisces	Aries	Taurus	Gemini
8am–10am	Aquarius	Pisces	Aries	Taurus
6am–8am	Capricorn	Aquarius	Pisces	Aries

Aries Rising

You're a natural-born leader and hate to follow, sometimes even putting yourself in the most awkward positions rather than admit you're wrong! But you're confident and ready to take on all comers. This makes you attractive to those around you, whether that's on a professional or personal level. In your younger years you're likely to be a bit of a tearaway and usually your family and friends will have the stories to back that one up! Your life's lesson is to get along with others, to include them in your decision making and to make sure that in relationships you give as well as receive love. Remember, you're an initiator, you don't stand around waiting for things to happen – you're the cause!

Taurus Rising

If this sign is rising, your chart is ruled by Venus, and being under her dominion you're likely to be attractive in an abundant way. Probably no size zero, you will like to eat and enjoy the occasional drink or two, and being comfortable is your aim. Quality of life is important to you but so is quality *in* your life, and seeing the difference could be a life lesson – is it more important to be happy or to have shiny things that confirm your status? You're cautious, a builder and planner, someone who takes their time, often to the frustration of those around you, but in love, oh in love you're hard to beat – a sensuous, touchy-feely type with a real appreciation of the finer things in life!

Gemini Rising

Hold the phone, it's a Gemini Rising with all the gossip! Chatty and ready to dish the dirt, you're there with your phone in one hand, BlackBerry in the other, and if you could you would be typing and sending e-mail with your feet – multi-tasking, multi-talented and ready to get things moving, shall we, shall we, come on, move it! Calm down, your remit in life may be to understand what you are talking about rather than repeat what you have seen or heard from others, to truly have knowledge rather than just words. You don't want to be tied down to one thing and you're best employed somewhere where you can do 100 things at once – magazines and television suit you well, for obvious reasons!

Cancer Rising

With your gentle rising sign, when you approach a group of people you won't storm in making your presence felt, you'll scuttle from side to side getting the measure of everyone before truly coming into your own, and that's when the claws can come out! Defensive of family and home, you will stick to the rules, and in relationships will have a set of expectations that must be fulfilled. You are here to learn how to put structure around yourself and to find stability in your home as well as within your family, and that can sometimes mean that you have issues with family, for how are you going to learn if you don't have the scenarios to learn from? Marriage is a very serious thing for you. So it should be, but more so for you than any other rising sign.

Leo Rising

Is that a spotlight? It will be shining on you, Leo Rising, and as long as your hair is looking fabulous, you'll be OK with that! Ready to perform at any time, you don't know if your drama is going to be a comedy or a thriller, but you just don't care as long as you are in the middle of it! You can be a little bossy on occasion and if you're not in charge it seems that nobody else can be. You're likely to be quite argumentative with those who think they can tell you what to do. You're also highly creative, wonderfully entertaining and amazingly talented, so find somewhere to show it all off! You're here to learn independence, to learn to stand out rather than lead (there is a difference) and to be unique.

Virgo Rising

Order your soya milk, decaffeinated coffee and settle in, Virgo Rising! You're very conscious of your body, what goes in it and what it's trying to tell you with that rash – no, it is a rash, I'm telling you, it *is* a rash – or that cough you have developed! Health is paramount and keeping it means routine: yoga, eating wholefoods, you name it, you're into it if it's going into you! You can attract people who are in need of support, those who want to talk things through and feed your desire to be the one making it all better for them. You have a quiet charm that will put itself out to help others and there's a side to you that wishes everyone and everything could just get along. Your life's lesson is letting go of the worry and realizing it will all be OK in the end. Honest.

Libra Rising

You are attractive – not necessarily good looking, before you go puffing yourself up, but attractive in that people are drawn to you because you exude niceness, and what a lovely word that is! Of course, as with most things, look underneath the niceness and you see a mechanism that generates being liked by everyone regardless of how you truly feel about things, and that means eventually that the niceness is replaced by the change of mind, the 'never wanted this in the first place' and the slamming door on the way out! Your life's lesson is to try to be more assertive, even if in the first instance you upset some people in the process. But of course this rising sign can work for you professionally. Choose the law, counselling – anywhere you have to see two sides but aren't directly involved!

Scorpio Rising

Power is what rises from you, Scorpio Rising. When you walk into a room you may not be the loudest person in there, but you're certainly noticed. The original strong silent type, you give off an aura of authority and purpose. You're the Marmite of rising signs and people will love you or hate you, but they will have an opinion and that's all that matters – they are talking about you. You may be a security freak with more locks on your doors than most, but the truth is you value your privacy and sometimes you need to withdraw completely, even switching the phone off in the middle of a working day because you need your precious space. Your life's lesson is about being cuddly. Yes, feeling emotion and expressing it – scary, isn't it?

Sagittarius Rising

And another thing I can do for you is to plan the event whilst riding round on a unicycle balancing a cream cracker on my head – oh really? Making great big promises that may be too tough to keep is a trait of this rising sign, but we all know your heart is in the right place, it's just your brain seems to have lost its way! Of course, you wouldn't have got into a fix if you hadn't offered your services in the first place, but you just can't help yourself and that's the problem! Stand back, slow down and think before you decide what you want to do – that's one of your life's lessons – and then once you do know what you're going to do, get someone else to help you, someone you know will finish the job, because you won't! At least you have a great sense of humour – you'll need it!

Capricorn Rising

Are you having a good time? You want to tell your face! Breaking into a smile may not be how you show you're having a good time – inside you're laughing yourself silly, you just don't see why you have to be rolling about guffawing all of the time, and frankly you are a very funny person. Yes, you are, but one of those straight-faced funny people. You're the serious one, the one who carries the passports on holiday, the one who checks the car before you go anywhere, the one who takes on all the responsibility for everything and everyone. You're big on family and life's lesson for you is providing for that family.

Just remember to take some time to enjoy them too.

Aquarius Rising

You stand out in a crowd, you're unique and the one most people would describe as unusual! It may be your love of all things scientific and geeky, or perhaps it's your unusual dress code, or maybe your freaky hair – it's going somewhere, trust me – but whatever it is, you're here to make us all think outside the box. You can come up with solutions nobody else would have thought of and they seem to work when you do. You also get on well in a team as long as you are given space to have your say – never ever should you be told to be quiet! Of course you can be cantankerous, too, and if someone says you must turn right you will of course turn left just to annoy them. You are hard to pin down and box, and that's because you shouldn't be – the freer, the better. You tend to love travel and are a great watcher of humanity. Your life lesson is to learn to go with the flow, to let go of restrictions and trust that all will be well. You currently have Neptune and Jupiter in your first house, meaning opportunities are presenting themselves but you either don't see them or aren't sure if they are for you. You are like a bird whose cage door has been left open – do you fly or do you stay in the safety of where you are?

Pisces Rising

You're not one for bucking the trend, in fact you're not really one for a trend in the first place, preferring to shuffle about in your own little world and change that world when you feel the need or the inclination. You get it, Pisces Rising, you get the fact that nothing is ultimately that important and everything changes in time. You don't want to know the facts, you just want to know how something makes you feel, and your intuition is incredibly accurate. You have a way about you that's almost magical, an aura that attracts others to you as if you have cast a spell that enchants and intrigues those around you. Your life's lesson, however, is about facing up to those facts you avoid so beautifully.

Remember to Put It All Together...

If you have my other books you'll now know your Sun sign, where your north and south nodes are and where Saturn is in your chart. Add this information as well as your personality Sephira to the mix and you'll start to see a picture develop right in front of your eyes. Exciting times!

Chapter 11

Onwards and Upwards

S o where next? All the methods, ideas and information in this book may be interesting, but are you ready to begin integrating your higher self into your life in a more obvious way, and by obvious I don't mean so others can see it, I mean so you can see how it can affect your life for the better?

And if you are, how do you go about doing it? I wish there was one answer I could give here, and one for each and every e-mail or enquiry I get, or even one for every ten, but all of us are unique and that means that only you have the answer that's right for you right now and the best person to find it is you. But it takes work.

This where we sometimes fall down. We all have plenty of work to be getting on with as it is, but this is work that's about the soul, work that comes from the soul and returns its rewards to the soul, and what greater prize can there be than knowing you did well, knowing you sorted it out, knowing that you Knew Yourself so much more today than you did yesterday?

Some people will tell you it's not worth it, some will tell you it's nonsense and some will tell you that you can't change anything as it's all written in stone anyway, so why bother? But that's just some people. *Some.* Not you, not me, just some: So Over-Meddling Energies. But when you're dealing with other people it may be best to think about whom you tell and what you tell them. Silence can often be your best defence, which is why the psychic arts were often hidden and all the more powerful for it.

But whatever you do and whichever path you choose, remember you are part of the divine and as part of it you can never be anything other than divine. That's the best secret of all.

**Blessed Be
David Wells**

Appendix

Earth Energies

Tony Ainsworth

There is a very simplistic approach available to take with Earth energy and that's if it's not balanced, it's wrong, and the ultimate ambition of any Earth energy practitioner is to achieve perfect balance of Earth energy in buildings, spaces or areas and ultimately in people.

Well, that's the simplicity sorted, now back to reality, and what you need to know to get that simplicity.

The yin/yang symbol shows balance but it also shows Earth energy has two 12-hour cycles and two different types. The tail of the white section starts at 2 a.m. and peaks at 2 p.m., while the dark section's tail starts at 2 p.m. and peaks at 2 a.m. The white portion of the sign refers to what's today known as Terrestrial magnetism, Tm, and the black portion of the sign refers to what we know today as radiation.

Tm comes from over a million lightning strikes a day hitting the Earth's surface somewhere and discharging millions of volts of electricity directly into the Earth's surface, and by the distance that energy travels the currents are reduced from millions of volts down to what's known today as Magneto-telluric (tiny magnetic) or Mt energy. Modern concerns about Mt energy came before the EU in its directive in 1999 and its amendments in 2004, 2007 and 2009 on Mt energy in the workplace as residual waste from electrical appliances. There is no concern about natural Mt strength or type anywhere else, as science is of the opinion that background Earth radiation and type are natural. This is because science still believes Terrestrial magnetism comes from the Earth's metal core, because in 1600 William Gilbert said so in a book and James Clerk Maxwell agreed with him 300 years later. It wasn't till the 1960s that the number of lightning strikes was recorded and no one bothered to change the theory of Terrestrial magnetism, which is still taught in our schools as factual science.

Radiation comes from the Earth's hot core and to create the required balance of these energies, as the yin/yang symbol also shows, is to keep them separate, because if these energies join, the result in scientific terms is ionizing radiation, which is also known as radon gas. The symptoms of long-term low-dose exposure to ionizing radiation are benign tumours, 39 forms of cancer, gastro-intestinal disorders, bacterial infection, electrolyte imbalance, cataracts and DNA damage. The diversity of symptoms does not end there, as the known psychological effects of moon phase are not included, nor is other activity associated with Earth energy when good and when bad. The type of experience Earth energy gives is simply good or bad depending on whether the ground is balanced or unbalanced. There is no difference between normal or paranormal in Earth energy, the effect perceived is related to the strength of Earth energy and the type in place, be it balanced or unbalanced.

The Earth has 14 different strength levels of Earth energy and we can't discount any, because none is a fixed width – both Tm and radiation fields vary in size over 24 hours – but if we take the eclipse of the sun in 1999, the physical event took only a few moments, but Earth energy changed a month before the event until the exact moment of eclipse and then reversed the cycle it had just completed, which took another month. What actually happened was that radiation fields from the Earth's core widened prior to the eclipse and Tm fields narrowed until the very moment of eclipse, when there was no visible evidence of any Tm field at all. Seconds later the Tm fields returned and started getting wider by the minute until everything was back to normal, whatever normal was for that month. Throughout the period I had done my job by keeping the two energies separate at all times until nature took over for one final moment and to this day I still don't know what happened to the Tm fields, all I cared about was that when they came back they were separate from the radiation fields.

The effect and cause of this event were planetary movement. David can predict major Earth energy changes by planetary movement and cycle, but the limitation of all astrology today is the historical and hidden presumption that all buildings are as balanced as they should be. Once they would have been, but today they clearly are not. The other restriction on astrology, like Earth energy, is that it's place specific.

Astronomy tells us a little about what's going on; astrology tells us the effect of that on the Earth and its population in a place-specific way. To highlight what I mean, the summer solstice on 21 June in the northern hemisphere is the end of the weakest cycle of the year – from 22 June Earth energy starts increasing. But if we were in Australia on 21 June, that would be the end of the strong period of Earth energy and on 22 June it would start weakening. In the northern hemisphere, Halloween, on 31 October, is the beginning of the next cycle of Earth energy increase, but in Australia it's the marker point for a further period of decrease. All points in between the northern and southern hemispheres have opposite Earth energy strengths and the least variable place on the planet is the equatorial regions. The strongest Earth energy is nearer the Earth's magnetic poles. Earth energy is not rocket science, really.

Balancing Earth energy is my day job in a nutshell. Whatever the challenge of the landscape is or a place is, it's my job to balance Earth energy as a first priority. The secondary part of that job is spirit release, whether spirit is evident or not, and I'm not confined to working in a building or place where there are health or paranormal problems or both. Most of my work is actually round the building or place I've been called into, and the area I'm interested in could be a mile or more round the property.

The object of treating the larger area is to take pressure off the building I'm dealing with. I'm not actually treating other buildings unless I have to, but to get the clients right I'm generally lifting the ambience or atmosphere in that area. It's not much good washing the windows if the house next door is on fire or there's a brush fire down the street. Of course, you can clean the windows in those conditions but very shortly they will need washing again, and so it is with Earth energy if you haven't used the right materials or understood that Earth disturbance unbalances buildings that have been treated in the past.

To treat Earth energy, historically Earth acupuncture was employed, using needles of wood or stone. To protect the area, ditches were used to keep the inside area protected from the Earth disturbance outside. If every building had its own henge (ditch), things might be a little less complex nowadays, but they haven't, and the simplicity of that situation is getting over it and then getting on with it.

Once the reader understands the problem, keeping any building or place balanced is key. Earth disturbance unbalances it and Bob the builder is ever-present these days, but earthquake or tremor has a very big impact, too, and the fact you cleaned your building or windows last year or last week does not mean you need never clean them again. The point I'm getting to slowly is the historical maintenance issue. If a building has been treated or balanced in the past and the owner or occupant thinks that is a lifetime treatment, they will be terribly wrong, because the only lifetime treatment of a building wasn't available anywhere until the late sixties and was only fully developed very recently.

The simple and permanent solution to balancing a property or place is the use of the right-size rare Earth magnets in the right place. And that's not really how simple it gets, but how complex.

Ordinary magnets do work placed in the right positions but not for long. Only rare Earth magnets come with the guarantee that the property will be treated in minutes, and the better news is anyone can fit them in their own property or workplace in seconds. Rare Earth magnets should be fitted in pairs, one to the rear of central-heating radiators on the far left-hand side and the other on the far right-hand side. The average cost of treating a building with a 5,000 square foot footprint is £20 (GBP), including post and packing.

The next problem is area, but with the right rare Earth magnets fitted to a vehicle, areas can be cleaned wherever the vehicle travels on normal business, so we supply magnets for one vehicle and eight radiators in the pack provided.

If you can't afford the pack, which many people sadly can't, the historical way of treating Earth energy was with magnetized water. If you 'acupuncture' the land correctly near a stream or river, that magnetizes the water and balances it, but the ancients often carved out 'cups' on standing stones and used the water in them to liven up wood or stone circles on a regular basis.

To treat any building or place using magnetized water, first acquire a plastic pot or glass container. An old soft drinks bottle complete with cap is ideal. Make a small hole in the cap and break a fridge magnet or any other magnet till it passes through the neck of the bottle. Fill it with water and its contents are ready to be sprinkled.

If there is some difficulty getting a magnet, salt can be used instead, but only use a teaspoon of salt in two litres of water – any more and you're wasting salt and it won't have the slightest difference in effect. Rock salt, table salt, road salt – all can be used, it makes not the slightest bit of difference.

If salt is added to water that's been magnetized, it increases the power of the water by a significant factor. There is a procedure to follow closely using salt, and that's to put the salt in the container first and add the water, being particularly careful that there is no contact between the liquid in the container and any metal, such as the tap perhaps.

Sprinkle the magnetized water lightly in all rooms, upstairs and down, and then go outside and treat the largest area possible. With a five-gallon container I once treated two islands using a vehicle and magnetized water because ordinary magnets didn't work as they hadn't enough power. It is very important to treat outside a property for two reasons: it gets you out of the building for a start and that will take pressure off the person involved; and the largest area needs treating. Anyway, that only takes a few minutes.

The next thing you should do is relax for a few moments outside the house/building. Take a few deep breaths, chill out and then enter the property slowly. Don't rush in, as you will likely miss the effect of balanced ground. The building will be strangely calm. The temperature in the house will have risen and the cold rooms and rooms you didn't like before will be peaceful. It is advisable to stand calmly in each room, close your eyes, breathe deeply and relax. The room should be very peaceful and you should become very relaxed. If there is the slightest hint of anxiety, treat the room with more water, and if it's an upstairs room, check the room below it and add a little more water and then leave the house to relax again. Check again in around ten minutes.

If there has been what people call paranormal activity, it is advisable in the first instance to switch all power off at the mains supply, treat the building with magnetized water and go out for a walk for an hour before returning. These aren't common situations, but it's better to know how to treat them than not know. In any situation you don't like or want to put up with, you have to take control of the ground you're standing on and the ground anything else is using or being trapped by.

There is not a man living or dead that's ever removed or released a spirit – spirit removes or releases spirit – but man can help by balancing the ground. There's the old joke I tell about a conversation I had with God. 'Will you help me win the lottery, Lord?' I asked. 'Of course,' he replied, 'but this time meet me halfway and buy a ticket, Tony.' If you want spirit removed, ask spirit to do it after you have balanced the ground. I know many mediums and psychics who can't see spirit in their own homes or don't have any idea that the energy in their homes is often appalling.

A later development, following on from magnetized water, is holy water. These are two entirely different liquids, but they have the same effect when used on the Earth and are undone by any Earth disturbance after use. Property or places treated with either should be treated at least three times a week as a maintenance measure, but only the ground floor of a building needs treating and the power supply need not be turned off in any further treatment to balance a building.

Prayer also works to balance Earth energy. It has to be specific, can be very short and can be practised standing up or on the back of a motorbike. The words 'clear', 'heal' and 'balance' must be used and the effect is likely to last until any Earth disturbance occurs. The number to call might not be in a book, but the lines are open 24/7 and there's no 'call waiting' nonsense.

If further help is required, that generally comes under the heading of healing, and a timely reminder is that prevention is far better than cure. Healing – conventional or alternative or both – is better practised on balanced ground, as is the patient's lifestyle, including sleeping arrangements, as Earth energy is stronger at night, whether it's balanced or unbalanced.

Alternative healers in particular often remove or replace energy, and that often falls, under the laws of gravity, to the floor, where everyone ignores it. If rare Earth magnets have been used, the energy will be rebalanced as it falls, as will any waste from electrical appliances in the building. If the building isn't balanced, magnetized water or holy water should be used between the first client and the next client to rebalance the mess on the carpet. In conventional medicine the use of defibrillators is common to restart the heart, and most doctors know the brain and muscles work off electrical signals, but tell a conventional practitioner there's a hole in your aura and you're likely to be sectioned. The simple facts are you can't have an electrical current without a magnetic field and anyone without an aura has passed away. If there is a hole in the aura there is weak or no current, and repairing the aura is far less effective than repairing the flow of current.

To make a cake the best ingredients should be selected with care and mixed carefully. As a healer of the old school myself, I use every means at my disposal for the benefit of the client. Faith, spiritual, colour, shamanic Reiki healing and on occasion natural regression are the ingredients a client needs, but the thing they need most of all is a balanced building to live in and a balanced building to work in, and the space in between the two buildings to be balanced.

It's not hard to change the world – all you need is enough Wells Angels on the case and the right rare Earth magnets.

Reading and Resources

○ The Order of the White Lion for teaching and information: www.orderofthewhitelion.com

○ Aristia for crystals, books and fabulousness: www.aristia.co.uk

○ A therapist in your area for past-life regression: www.pastliferegression.co.uk

○ Pure spirit for healing in Essex and beyond: www.purespirithealingcentre.com

○ Frankie Howerd OBE Trust for Frankie info: www.frankiehowerdobetrust.org

○ and me for – well, I'll leave that up to you! www.davidwells.co.uk

○ To learn more about Tony Ainsworth's work, please look for the link on my own website.

JOIN THE HAY HOUSE FAMILY

As the leading self-help, mind, body and spirit publisher in the UK, we'd like to welcome you to our family so that you can enjoy all the benefits our website has to offer.

 EXTRACTS from a selection of your favourite author titles

 COMPETITIONS, PRIZES & SPECIAL OFFERS Win extracts, money off, downloads and so much more

 LISTEN to a range of radio interviews and our latest audio publications

 CELEBRATE YOUR BIRTHDAY An inspiring gift will be sent your way

 LATEST NEWS Keep up with the latest news from and about our authors

 ATTEND OUR AUTHOR EVENTS Be the first to hear about our author events

 iPHONE APPS Download your favourite app for your iPhone

 HAY HOUSE INFORMATION Ask us anything, all enquiries answered

join us online at **www.hayhouse.co.uk**

 292B Kensal Road, London W10 5BE
T. 020 8962 1230 E: info@hayhouse.co.uk